EVANGELISM IS . . .

EVANGELISM IS . . .

Clinton M. Marsh

Geneva Press • Louisville, Kentucky

Scripture quotations from the New Revised Standard Version
of the Bible are copyright © 1989 by the Division of Christian Education
of the National Council of the Churches of Christ in the U.S.A.
and are used by permission.

Book and cover design by Jennifer K. Cox
Cover art: Crowd, *by Judy Byford. Courtesy of SuperStock.*

First edition
Published by Geneva Press
Louisville, Kentucky

This book is printed on acid-free paper that meets the
American National Standards Institute Z39.48 standard. ∞

PRINTED IN THE UNITED STATES OF AMERICA
98 99 00 01 02 03 04 05 06 — 10 9 8 7 6 5 4 3 2

Library of Congress Cataloging-in-Publication Data

Marsh, Clinton M. (Clinton McClurkin), date.
  Evangelism is . . . Clinton M. Marsh — 1st ed.
    p.   cm.
  Includes bibliographical references.
  ISBN 0-664-50013-7
  1. Evangelistic work. 2. Witness bearing (Christianity)
  I. Title.
  BV3790.M38 1997
  269'.2—DC21   97-25542

I gratefully dedicate *Evangelism Is . . .* to the memory of the late Dr. Addison H. Leitch, scholar, preacher, theologian, educator. It was "Ad" who, doing Bible studies at a New Wilmington (Pennsylvania) missionary conference about forty years ago, sparked my interest in the story of Jesus and the Samaritan woman at the wall at Sychar and launched me on a lifetime of study and use of that conversation.

I dedicate this book also to the Witherspoon United Presbyterian Church of Indianapolis, Indiana, where for eighteen years we sat together under the instruction of the Holy Spirit and under the guidance of that same Spirit sought to be practitioners and messengers of the love that drives true evangelism.

Contents

Preface

In 1963, after eighteen years as pastor of an African American Presbyterian church that grew from about one hundred members to more than eight hundred, I was called to serve on the national evangelism staff of The United Presbyterian Church in the United States of America. Serving two years there and five years in Africa, and serving with the evangelism portfolio in two synods, stretched my evangelism service to twelve years.

Working for those twelve years in evangelism at the national and synod levels of the church, I grew into a painful awareness that there was something dreadfully amiss in the life of evangelism in the denomination. The signs of this were in the congregations, at every governing level, and in the seminaries, where courses on evangelism were being dropped. Colleagues from other denominations reported similar patterns.

The steady and frightening shrinkage of some denominations has caused a sense of unease that is giving rise to at least lip service to evangelism. At the same time, the unbelievable deterioration of the state of society, in this nation and in the world, is provoking a new look at the need for religious faith and, to some extent, of the need for the church. The current malaise may be providing openings for the Holy Spirit to redirect the life of the church and its members. This book seeks to offer help at both simple and deeper levels for searching Christians, both lay and clergy.

Our discussion of evangelism is oriented around Jesus' having chosen to go through Samaria, and around John's record of the events there. This Gospel record has proved many times to be an effective vehicle in workshops, conferences, and lectures to disarm negative concepts of what evangelism is.

Although my experiences as an evangelist and instructor in evangelism have been in Presbyterian denominations, the similarities in trends between Presbyterians and some other denominations have been so striking that the book might as well be written for them. It should be of use generally, and not only to the churches with problems of diminishing membership. The principles gleaned from the event at the well in Samaria are valid for any who are looking for fresh concepts on the subject of evangelism.

Simplicity of language and down-to-earth illustrations seek to emulate Jesus' style of teaching. To aid those who are keenly interested in evangelism but not deeply versed in scripture, there are copious Bible references. The book is thus a Bible course and a homiletic sourcebook.

To aid those who have had no experience in planned, organized evangelistic work, it outlines practical guidance for the congregation. It seeks to display how every aspect of church life and every organization and member of the church relates to evangelism. Those people who do not feel capable of explaining the message of salvation may find their roles as choir members, ushers, members of the property committee, or just plain members in the pew. All can be members of the evangelism team.

Evangelism Is . . . seeks to help persons to understand Why? Who? How? When? and sometimes, Why not?

The underlying theme (in words not original with me) is as follows: "Love is the motive; love is the message; love is the method." In this book, we will deal with the motive, the message, and the method.

I am aware that there have been many and profound cultural changes since my days as a pastor. Yet I believe there are some basic continuities in human nature and society, so that old principles may not be displaced entirely by new, but have continued relevance.

I acknowledge my indebtedness:

To my wife, Agnes, whose life and work in the church, coupled with her career as an English teacher, enabled her to contribute to both form and content;

To Roland Tapp, who coached me in many unfamiliar aspects of authorship and publication;

To former evangelism staff colleague and competent pastor Bruce Coleman, who read the manuscript and made many recommendations;

To Fred Page, my counselor on aspects relating to the small church, who enriched the content greatly;

To several others who evaluated chapters relating to their special proficiencies;

And to the countless people whose names I do not remember who, during and after seminars and workshops, contributed pertinent thoughts about the event at the well.

HOW WE
GOT HERE

Is it possible that some parts of the Christian church have no future? It is quite common for someone to survey a denomination's statistics, project them into the future, and cynically predict the year of that denomination's demise. Fortunately this is fallacious, making no allowance for the work of the Holy Spirit, but it dramatizes the seriousness of what is happening in the lives of several historically strong denominations.

There has been a disturbing similarity in the overall trends in a number of the historic churches. Statistics below from the Presbyterian Church (U.S.A.) and its antecedent churches illustrate what is disturbingly general.

In the former United Presbyterian Church in the U.S.A. (UPCUSA), the national staff used to chronicle the post-World War II record as the periods of:

> Increase
>
> Increase of the increase
>
> Decrease of the increase
>
> Decrease
>
> Increase of the decrease

The church is seeking to reach the period of the decrease of the decrease, with increase seemingly a long way off. The similarity of the pattern of the Presbyterian Church in the United States (PCUS) prior to

Statistical Table 1.
UPCUSA 1973–1982/PCUSA 1983–1995

Year	Congregations	Members	Loss	Professions	Average	Adult Baptisms	Average	Infant Baptisms	Average	Deaths	Average
1973	8,742	2,817,052		+		12,799	1.4	39,097	4.4	36,114	4.1
1974	8,719	2,731,538	85,514			12,936	1.4	37,763	4.3	34,157	3.9
1975	8,686	2,665,970	65,568			12,785	1.2	37,612	4.3	34,254	3.9
1976	8,675	2,615,659	50,311			13,179	1.5	36,395	4.2	34,010	3.9
1977	8,656	2,569,404	46,225			11,721	1.3	36,937	4.2	32,858	3.8
1978	8,627	2,520,334	49,070			10,943	1.1	36,139	4.2	33,885	3.9
1979	8,694	2,477,331	43,003			11,174	1.2	37,830	4.3	32,245	3.8
1980	8,832	2,424,020	43,311	58,588	6.6	12,236	1.3	36,898	4.4	33,473	4.0
1981	8,993	2,387,869	46,151	58,430	6.4	12,804	1.4	39,498	4.3	32,848	3.7
1982	8,975	2,351,106	36,763	57,174	6.1	13,773	1.4	40,128	4.4	32,412	3.6
1983	11,662	3,166,764	*Reunion*	69,863	5.9	16,996	1.4	50,785	4.4	42,898	3.7
1984	11,639	3,100,941	30,287	69,907	6.0	16,534	1.4	50,507	4.3	43,270	3.7
1985	11,621	3,057,216	43,725	65,783	5.6	18,826	1.4	49,712	4.2	43,007	3.7
1986	11,598	3,016,478	40,738	64,645	5.5	15,615	1.3	49,039	4.2	42,979	3.7
1987	11,573	2,976,927	39,551	61,652	5.3	14,729	1.2	48,580	4.2	42,845	3.7
1988	11,593	2,938,820	38,107	61,236	5.2	14,300	1.2	47,978	4.2	43,175	3.7
1989	11,537	2,905,696	33,124	62,350	5.4	14,725	1.2	49,849	4.2	42,531	3.7
1990	11,501	2,866,703	38,993	99,128	7.6*	14,209	1.2	49,018	4.3	41,469	3.6
1991	11,468	2,825,035	41,668	99,384	8.6*	14,110	1.2	46,744	4.0	41,640	3.6
1992	11,456	2,790,396	34,639	100,014	8.7*	14,449	1.2	45,017	3.9	40,362	3.5
1993	11,416	2,742,192	48,204	94,594	8.1*	13,552	1.1	42,080	3.7	41,358	3.7
1994	11,399	2,708,252	33,940	96,450	8.4*	13,652	1.2	41,163	3.6	41,386	3.6
1995	11,361	2,665,276	32,986	94,561	8.3*	12,979	1.1	40,375	3.5	41,079	3.6
CUMULATIVE AVERAGES							1.3		4.1		3.7

+ Profession of faith figures were not reported until 1980

* A change in means of reporting makes this figure meaningless for comparisons

Averages are per church per year for professions, adult baptisms, and infant baptisms.

Statistical Table 2.
PCUS 1973–1982

Year	Congregations	Professions	Average	Adult Baptisms	Average	Infant Baptisms	Average
1973	4,347	19,991	4.6	6,095	1.4	10,694	2.4
1974	4,117	18,209	4.4	6,040	1.4	9,998	2.4
1975	4,028	18,010	4.5	5,968	1.5	9,994	2.5
1976	4,036	16,625	4.1	5,589	1.4	9,960	2.4
1977	4,010	17,043	4.2	5,079	1.2	10,218	2.5
1978	4,007	15,744	3.9	4,908	1.2	10,489	2.6
1979	4,067	15,973	3.9	4,877	1.2	10,586	2.5
1980	4,159	17,394	4.1	5,493	1.2	11,620	2.8
1981	4,174	17,159	4.1	5,557	1.2	12,183	2.9
1982	4,250	19,974	4.4	5,367	1.2	12,069	2.8
CUMULATIVE AVERAGE			4.1		1.3		2.6

Deaths were not reported.
Averages are per church per year for professions, adult baptisms, and infant baptisms.

reunion both in gross statistics and in various other categories is eerily similar, as may be seen in table 2. The reunited church has merely continued the pattern.

We may dramatize the history of the two churches that now constitute the Presbyterian Church (U.S.A.). In 1958, when the Presbyterian Church U.S.A. and the United Presbyterian Church of North America united, the new United Presbyterian Church in the U.S.A. (UPCUSA) had a membership of 3,159,562. At that time, the Presbyterian Church in the United States (PCUS) had a membership of 848,738—a total of 4,008,300 in the two churches. In 1983, when the UPCUSA and PCUS reunion took place, the combined membership was 3,166,764. The total membership had been reduced by 841,536, the loss being nearly the equivalent of the total PCUS membership in 1958.

As of 1995, the figure was 2,665,276. That is a reduction of 1,343,024 over the thirty-seven-year period from the 1958 merger.

The statistical tables of the two churches from 1973 to the present show the nature of the reductions. They show:

1. the declining membership year by year
2. the low level of professions of faith
3. the low level of adult baptisms
4. the low level of infant baptisms
5. the comparison of offsetting deaths

In no year did the denominations have as many as two adult baptisms per congregation per year, and professions of faith were minimal. This is to say that instead of reaching people for the gospel, any growth claimed was similar to playing "musical chairs," not to pioneer evangelism.

There are those who discount the importance of this trend, saying that one cannot measure the strength of a church by statistics, cynically referring to it as "the old numbers game." It is true that large numbers do not necessarily mean a healthy church, as we shall see later, nor do small numbers necessarily signal ineffectiveness, but statistics can be revealing.

While "good" statistics can be deceiving and even dangerous, other types of statistics can also send messages. When my temperature was 103 degrees one morning, it was just a "statistic," but it was one that told me that somewhere in my body something had gone awry. The statistics of some of our denominations are like that; they sound serious warnings.

We must recognize the fact that some particular congregations are in situations where growth is hardly possible, and with many there is no alternative to shrinkage. But when a denomination of more than eleven thousand congregations, scattered over the nation in all kinds of settings, shows steady and continued decline for decades amidst a growing national population, it is necessary to examine what the symptoms mean.

Statistics can certainly cloud our understanding. The church does not measure success by members, money, and property. God's admonition to Samuel, sent to find a successor to Saul as king—". . . the LORD does not see as mortals see; they look on the outward appearance, but the LORD looks on the heart" (1 Sam. 16:7)—is valid in evaluating the church as well as individuals. While certain statistics are symptoms of illness, statistics that look healthy are not necessarily symptoms of health.

Post–World War II statistics were great; most denominations grew incredibly. Those were exciting years, even though some leaders warned that we should not be too sanguine. They cautioned that it was not all healthy growth. But who could argue with success?

There were psychological factors that contributed to that rapid growth. Having won the war, there was a feeling of compulsion to thank God, and turning to the church was part of it. On the other hand, the trauma represented by gold stars in windows and the broken bodies, shattered minds, and what the horribleness of the war said about the nature of humanity left many drained and groping. They needed some "invisible means of support." They, too, turned to the church.

The echo of the guns and bombs of the war had barely ceased when the nation was thrown into a "cold war." An ally suddenly became a deadly enemy. Engaged in a life-or-death struggle with "godless communism," it seemed only right to many in America that they should be aligned with the major identifiable "God-related" agency. So, they turned to the church. Maybe it was faith, maybe it was an unconscious superstition, but they came.

A second factor was demographic and sociological. It was the era of the suburban explosion, and the phrase "mushroom growth" was apt. Almost as those fungi appear overnight, thousands of communities appeared as if by magic. As in the nineteenth century some denominations accompanied western expansion with churches, they now moved with this new frontier. Thoughtful developers included places for churches in their plans. In many communities, the church was the only community organization and facility, and churches were truly community centers. It was at the churches that children's and youth activities took place. At the churches one met neighbors and forged friendships. To "join it" seemed just natural, especially if one was impelled by the force of the psychological factors which were in play.

A New Evangelism Method

This was the setting into which a new evangelistic method came into play, or, at least, when an old one was rediscovered. It was the two-by-two lay visitation program, modeled after Jesus' training his disciples and sending them out in pairs. The National Council of Churches' department of evangelism published excellent training materials. Filmstrips, turnover charts, texts, manuals, files, prospect and decision cards—all the best tools of the day were in service. The National Council staff was available for leadership training. Denominations added their own materials and staff and funneled training to the lower units and the congregations. It was a wonderful and exciting time.

What happened to it?

To a large extent it went sour in the making. It called for careful, prayerful, biblically based training of those who went out on behalf of the church. But the fields were so ripe for harvest that there was no time (or need?) to waste in training workers! Many new churches were filled with new Christians who had no depth or biblical background. In many older churches, few members had enough grounding in the gospel to be ready to converse with people about the meaning of the faith. Many pastors did not even know how to define evangelism and were totally unequipped to do the training essential for representing, not just the church, but Christ and the gospel.

The result was that what should have been a surge of evangelism became in many instances merely a massive membership recruitment binge. People who were supposed to be witnesses to the faith were salespeople for the church. Some who visited homes on behalf of the church emphasized the fine scouting activities, the wonderful music, and the fellowship. It was documented that some even pointed out that the prospective members were new in the community and the church was the place to make business contacts. "Our pastor is a regular guy" was code for, "You don't need to be too concerned about any change of lifestyle."

Certainly there was much good work done. Many earnest pastors and laypeople grew in their understanding of basic religious truth as they schooled themselves to interpret it to those who often were beginners. The ability to listen as others expressed their beliefs and questions and to reply with sensitivity and meaning grew with practice. In some congregations, new members received training and were exposed to constant preaching and teaching that anchored them in the faith. Where these things happened, not only did churches grow in numbers, but people and churches grew in spiritual power.

Village Church (Presbyterian) in Prairie Village, Kansas, was born in this era, and the Holy Spirit used the lay visitation movement with such great results that it is one of the largest and strongest churches in the denomination today. Many other churches, large and small, witnessed spiritual growth and power.

In many churches this solid work was not done, and members were just recruited. With people flooding into congregations poorly instructed, coming biblically illiterate and remaining so, burgeoning statistics were often cancerous growth. This is where statistics were deceiving. And worst of all, needy souls were betrayed. As someone expressed it, "The hungry sheep look up and are not fed."

Jesus warned in the parable of the sower (Matt. 13:1–9 et al.) about seed sown in shallow or rocky soil, that it responded quickly but withered just as rapidly. This was the story in thousands of cases.

In the UPCUSA, many remained on the rolls until the per capita assessments forced congregations to assess their membership more realistically. As they studied their rolls, they found they were paying assessments for masses of missing persons. Finding it easier to remove their names than to search for and seek to reclaim them, roll clearing contributed to the first waves of membership reductions in the denomination. It was not, however, a loss of *members*, except in a statistical sense—as disciples, many had never been there.

At the risk of sounding cynical, I will add that a more lasting problem was that many of them stayed. They had come with little understanding of the gospel. They were received casually. Serious study of scripture and the faith was not provided. Where, in addition, preaching was superficial, the nurture that might have helped them to grow in the faith was missing. But many were people of intelligence, competence, and leadership ability, so they became teachers, leaders, and elders, entrusted with the spiritual leadership of the congregations. The cynical statement that there are elders and other church leaders who have to look in the table of contents to find Genesis in the Bible is a statement nearer the truth than one would like to think. And some went on to become ministers.

Church members and leaders who were "recruited" without an understanding of the gospel, and who didn't acquire this later, would never be the leaders who would have the spiritual dynamism essential for real evangelism. The "recruited" can, at best, only be recruiters—never evangelists. But many of them hold the positions that should be leading the churches in devout outreach.

Thus that exciting postwar church growth set in motion waves in the life of the church whose negative impact can still be felt decades later and whose long-range effect is yet to be seen. But they were good "statistics."

That sudden growth is part of the story, but what else accounts for this steady and seemingly unstoppable decline? Especially when some denominations with different theological stances, different worship patterns, different demands of lifestyle, and other variances have grown steadily, and some of them rapidly?

Obviously, the reasons are many and varied. They are theological, cultural, historical. They involve human weakness and sinfulness. It is essential that we identify salient ones.

A False Explanation

A widely spread claim, unfortunately accepted by many, is that denominations that are losing members have focused too much on social concerns or the ills of society. In the past half century there has been a stronger sense in the mainstream churches of mission to society. In reaction, well-financed groups, whose very wealth raises questions about the society, led in the accusation that the church was too much involved in the issues of the world, to the neglect of evangelism. There was hostility especially to the church's seeking to affect the structures of society.

Half of that accusation was true—there is no question that evangelism was neglected at many levels. But to relate it to too much investment in social concerns is completely false. Still, it created disharmonies in the denominations and made its contribution to the shrinking memberships. Perhaps the most damaging result of this misleading propaganda was that, in accepting it, many in the church did not seek the real reasons for the slide in church membership.

That propaganda was defective theology, in that it separated witness by the word from witness by the deed, when the two are inextricably intertwined. Often the word of love cannot be heard or understood unless accompanied by the actions of love. Medical people fought the bubonic plague and malaria unsuccessfully until they conquered the plagues of rats and fleas. Seeking the salvation of souls while neglecting the destructive nature of the society is often equally ineffective. Saving souls without saving the environment can be equally difficult.

A small boy from a home without a father used to bring his toys to my office so that I could play with him. When in youth club his teacher talked (in preinclusive days) about God as "Father," and he had no experience with a father, the relation with the pastor may have helped him to understand. It is often necessary for the church to interpret its language by its life.

The social action accusation is a completely false explanation of the diminishing church membership.

Uncertain Theology

A sure major contributor to the absence of evangelistic activity and effectiveness was and is shaky theology. Rigid theological dogmatisms have their shortcomings, but dealing with issues of faith and life with "on the one hand . . . , but on the other" theology can only make for weak Christians and inadequate church members.

A "cafeteria" theology, with no firm "Thus says the Lord," is not the basis for enthusiastic evangelism.

Preaching must cover many aspects of faith and ethics, but it should always be based on a commitment to Christ, the Savior of the world.

Christian education must address a wide range of life concerns, but it must be *Christian* education.

Counseling will use the best that psychology, psychiatry, and other sciences can provide. But while it will never be just "take your troubles to Jesus," it will be technical counseling placed within the context of a firm faith.

These are components of evangelism, because if all aspects of the life of the church are suffused with a strong belief that Christ is the answer to the issues of life, it is likely that there will be a serious concern with sharing that faith.

An experience from childhood will help to illustrate this. When toys were scarce and children had to find ways to entertain themselves, my brothers and I used to take a flashlight lens and focus it on a dry leaf or a piece of paper. The concentrated heat would set the object aflame. The diffused rays of the sun provided warmth for everything in sight, but it took a concentrating agent to produce fire. Just so, theological generalities may produce warmth, but never enough heat to fire the boilers to produce the steam to run the engines of evangelism

Several researchers claim that the people who are actually leaving the church are generally not going to any other church but are blending into secularism. This suggests that what they had grasped was so vaporous that it left them with nothing that would even cause them to look elsewhere for something more substantive.

Inadequate Concern
for Humanity

God was motivated by a concern for a broken, tragic humanity. When Jesus wept over Jerusalem, it was God weeping over the tragedy of human life and human lives (Matt. 23:37–39). There is little indication that Christians are agonizing over the tragedies that surround us. Earlier, in some churches more than in others, evangelistic motivation was in saving souls from hell and for heaven. Ministers and missionaries were sent westward with the expanding population and around the world to "save lost souls from hell." Never the highest motivation, hell has virtually disappeared from the preaching and teaching of the church. With it went some of the urgency about bringing Christ to bear upon the lives of people.

Spiritual and
Ecclesiastical History

The histories of various denominations contribute to their attitudes toward evangelism. The Presbyterian Church, developing in Scotland, was a family-centered church, promoting strong family worship and scripture reading. Much of its growth was from fairly large families. Scots, by nature, were a reserved people, not given to expressing their inner feelings. As the church developed in this country, this reserve continued and the expression "We raise our members," a kind of "biological evangelism," was often spoken, and it was the principle of action even when not consciously held. Now the infant baptism statistics reveal that cultural change has resulted in smaller families in the mid- dle- and upper-middle-class levels where Presbyterians cluster. There are, then, fewer children to sustain the rolls of the church, even if all of them became part of it.

That historical reserve continues through the life of the church to- day. A dismaying fact is that many Presbyterians, even those with sub- stantial faith and faith experience, shy away from witnessing to their beliefs in ways that would encourage others to consider that faith.

One hears the theologically unsound statement, "We don't talk about our faith; we live it and let that speak for us." How tragically right they are—it speaks for them, but unless they point to God, it goes no farther than their being seen as nice people! Jesus said, "Let your light shine before others, so that they may see your good works and give glory to your Father in heaven" (Matt. 5:16).

In addition, reaction to the ways that some others talk about their re- ligion drives them farther away from any easy expression of their own. They know that Jesus said, "You shall be my witnesses," but they pre- fer doing it corporately through the church—by the pastor.

Thus many Presbyterian congregations are deprived of the good that could result from their members' being scattered across the com- munity with friends, colleagues, and influence. A valuable source of spiritual power is lost.

Another fallacy is a sure overevaluation of the quality of the witness of their lives and of how others see them. The song "Let the Beauty of Jesus Be Seen in Me" is a valid prayer, expressing a desire that can never be fully realized. So there is a certain amount of arrogance in the claim that what others see in us is adequate to speak to them of Christ.

The protest "My faith is a private matter" is a way of defending be- ing mute. And Jesus has some words for mute Christians.

"Everyone therefore who acknowledges me before others, I also will acknowledge before my Father in heaven; but whoever denies me before others, I also will deny before my Father in heaven" (Matt. 10:32–33).

In the parable of the final judgment Jesus said that those who had fed and clothed the indigent and ministered to prisoners would find a welcome and those who had not would be rejected. Would those who had deprived the spiritually hungry of sustenance and the spiritual captives of freedom expect a warmer celestial welcome than those who had failed in material service?

Silent Christians prefer the way they do not witness to the ways some others do witness.

They seem not to relate the personal and societal brokenness all around them to the absence of Christ in the community's values and in lives.

They do not see that the "nicest" people and the worst people, alike, need Christ and that Christ can transform the lives of both.

These represent only some of the booby traps on the path of evangelism. A long and close look at Jesus' trip to Samaria and the events at the well and in the village can help to refocus the blurred vision that many have of evangelism.

As we look at the event at the well, we will see compulsion at work, the necessity of going out of the way, barriers being crossed, faith and patience at work, the truths of the gospel being shared, done passionately under the guidance and power of the Holy Spirit. And seen this way, evangelism may not seem so strange after all.

EVANGELISM IS ACTING UNDER COMPULSION OF LOVE

In the fourth chapter of his Gospel, John writes, "He left Judea and started back to Galilee. But he had to go through Samaria." However, Jesus did not have to go through Samaria. Although it was the most direct route, it was a route that few Jews took. Like other people who are afflicted with racial, religious, or other prejudices, Jews were willing to inconvenience themselves and go the long way. They would cross the Jordan and travel north or south through Peraea, and then recross the river, rather than have contact with the detested Samaritans. That hostility was so great that the Samaritan woman was surprised that Jesus even asked her for a drink of water.

If it was not travel convenience that caused him to lead his band through Samaria, what was it?

Jesus gave the answer to that question in John 3, in the conversation with Nicodemus. There he gave the heart of the gospel, saying that God's love had prompted God's reaching out to sinful humanity with an incredible mission. God's compulsion was love. Jesus' driving force was love. The love for humanity that brought him to earth was the same love that took him into Samaria.

Evangelism, being the continuation of Jesus' mission, must be the compulsion of love in action.

The incarnation of Jesus was a new act in the divine-human drama that began with creation and the human rejection of the very love that even now reaches out to rescue humanity from itself.

The drama began as Genesis tells of God's creating. It is not a scientific account, for the focus is not on the creation, but on the creator.

It gives us a picture of God creating carefully . . . creating patiently . . . creating lovingly.

There are those who, in their commitment to a literal interpretation of scripture, insist on a 144-hour-elapsed-time creation. In doing so they miss some of creation's glory. I have had repeated worshipful experiences, standing before my furnace with a lump of coal in my hand, thinking of the aeons that God took to develop that lump. How precious it was because of that long route through countless centuries to intercept my need! We identify miracles with the extraordinary and forget the miracle of the ordinary and dependable. We know what to expect of a grain of corn or an acorn planted in the earth. The smell of liver and onions, the taste of peach ice cream, the beauty of a sunset, the fascination of the combination of tone and rhythm—name your own earthly delights—are expressions of God's love in creation.

That love is shown in the intricacy of the universe, which permits the launching of an instrument toward some faraway spot in the heavens with the assurance that years later a heavenly body will be there for the rendezvous. That is now "ordinary." The dependability of the universe testifies to a God of love.

Not content with such lovely physical gifts, God placed human beings in community, giving us to one another in a relationship fashioned after the divine. "God is love" (1 John 4:8). "God created humankind in his image" (Gen. 1:27). Therefore, the nature of humanity was meant to be love, and love was meant to be the nature of human relationships. This was God's supreme gift to humanity in creation.

Rejection of that love was the first recorded human act, coming immediately after the account of creation. The placement of the record of the Fall signifies the fundamental role of that rejection in the tragic drama. Humanity ruptured its relationship with God, with itself, and with creation. This rebellion is the ingratitude shown to God for the carefully crafted setting, with its beauties of sense, order, and relationship.

Like the work of a master artist, with a few quick brush strokes the narrator portrays the beginning and spread of the human tragedy: the primary action in the garden (Gen. 3); the expansion into fratricide in the next generation (Gen. 4:1–16); and then alienation in society in the Babel event (Gen. 11:1–9).

That rebellion, the rejection of love, resulted in alienation from

God in the death God had promised. Inner alienation erupted as each person, having lost love, suffered self-hatred. Self-deprived of God (love), the people were unable to sustain harmonious interpersonal relationships. The Tower of Babel continues the chain relation of loveless living. The absence of true love led them into the kinds of wrong motivations and social disorientations that have perpetually frustrated loveless people from succeeding in their best efforts.

God's Response
to Human Rejection

But God had plan B—still love in action. The Old Testament gives glimpses of God's patient efforts to begin reconciliation. During those centuries, God was preparing for the dramatic intervention, the cosmic detour, the traumatic cross, and the victory over the death that humanity had so assiduously courted. God was developing a people from primitive tribalism to the ethical stage where Jesus could plant the seed of God's reconciliation.

That reconciliation focused in the incredible truth that Jesus gave to Nicodemus: "For God so loved the world that he gave his only Son, so that everyone who believes in him may not perish but may have eternal life" (John 3:16). God's love had come to earth in visible form and action.

A little boy told his mother that he had learned about Moses at Sunday school—how Moses had used engineers to build bridges for the Israelites and bombers to destroy Pharaoh's army. Challenged by his mother, he admitted that the teacher hadn't told it just that way, but that if she had heard the way the teacher told it, she would never believe it. The event at the Red Sea was one in a series of incredible events leading up to the most incredible of all—the incarnation and the resurrection.

Familiarity with the incredible dulls the excitement of it. Few citizens can tell who the first astronauts were, and fewer still the date that a man walked on the moon—events that were incredible for virtually all of human history and were doubted as impossible even as they took place.

The *good news* has become stale news to those who ought to be excitedly telling it.

There are several aspects of the compulsion. One is internal. The compulsion of evangelism must be the love of God empowering those whose lives have been effectively touched by it, eagerly sharing it with others. True evangelism will result in many people becoming members of the church, but church membership is not the goal of true evangelism. Evangelism is God's love passing through one life to another.

Electric power passes through a cord en route to some appliance that will use it. If there is a defect in the cord, not only does it fail to provide the implement with the needed power, it makes a short circuit, which is dangerous and can cause an expensive or even fatal fire. A defective Christian not only fails to witness, but can be the source of damage.

To understand this "love" we must rescue it from the quagmire of the English language in which one four-letter word is used for everything from the "agape," the divine love of God, to the lowest animal lusts. As in this book the effort is not to define evangelism, but to describe it in action, Paul, writing to the troubled church at Corinth, sought in the thirteenth chapter of his first letter to describe love in terms of human interactions and relationships.

We must separate it from the idea that love is the ultimate of like— if one likes something greatly, one loves it. "Like" implies being satisfied with something or someone. But God likes neither the world, nor you or me. However, God loves the world, you, and me in spite of the divine dissatisfaction with us. God was so displeased with the world that the cross was necessary. God loved the world so much that the cross was necessary. God wants the best for us in spite of ourselves. Our love must be like that. Jesus gave the key when he said, "Love your enemies and pray for those who persecute you." Our love in no way depends on their worthiness.

Another compulsion arises from our being Godlike in another way. When Jesus wept over Jerusalem he was demonstrating God's agony over God's broken world. We mentioned earlier that much of the compulsion for facing people with the gospel was eschatological: people must accept Christ to be saved for heaven or saved from hell. Jonathan Edwards's eighteenth-century sermon "Sinners in the Hands of an Angry God" used the description of the horrors of hell to stir people into accepting Christ, and such preaching stirred missionaries, ministers, and evangelists to accompany the westward sweep in this nation to save "sinners," and to spread around the globe to save the "heathen" from a burning hell.

Homiletics and hymnody were united in the message. Hymns like "Almost Persuaded" made fervent pleas to accept Christ. One stanza illustrates its message:

> "Almost persuaded," harvest is past!
> "Almost persuaded," doom comes at last!
> "Almost" cannot avail; "Almost" is but to fail!
> Sad, sad that bitter wail,
> "Almost"—but lost.
>
> (Philip P. Bliss)

The intensity of hell theology varied with denominations, but it was a universal factor. The thought of people spending eternity in a burning hell because nobody told them about Christ was a driving force, stimulating people to pray for mission, to give for mission, and to encourage their sons and daughters to go to distant and often dangerous lands in the service of an evangelistic mission.

That spirit is portrayed by a popular and traditional missionary hymn:

> O Zion, haste, thy mission high fulfilling,
> To tell to all the world that God is light;
> That he who made all nations is not willing
> One soul should perish, lost in shades of night.
>
> Behold, how many thousands still are lying
> Bound in the darksome prison house of sin,
> With none to tell them of the Savior's dying,
> Or of the life he died for them to win.
>
> Publish glad tidings, tidings of peace,
> Tidings of Jesus, redemption and release.
>
> (Mary A. Thomson)

The passion of that hymn captures the real spirit of evangelism and mission of the churches in an earlier day. It was a life-or-death theology.

It is not unusual today to hear the foreign mission movement debunked as merely an accessory to the spread of imperialism and economic exploitation. Like others, many missionaries were unable to keep faith and culture separate, but there was an integrity at the movement's core. I visited a cemetery at Libreville, Gabon, West Africa, where the Presbyterian Church had done mission work. Numerous missionaries were buried there. I was struck by the dates on their grave markers. First, they showed that all of them were young couples in their twenties. More piercing was the proximity of their arrival dates to the dates of their deaths. They had no knowledge of, immunity against, or medication for malaria, and it laid them low in waves. But they kept coming, drawn by their dedication to the saving of souls.

In a number of denominations today, hell, never the best motivation for evangelism, is no longer a compelling force behind it.

Whatever the beliefs about an eschatological hell, the world is replete with existential hells. God agonizes over these private, social, and structural hells. The chain-reaction crack-up—alienating humanity from God, self-alienation, interpersonal alienation, social alienation, and alienation from the universe—has produced a multiplicity of hells. There are hells of one's own creation, hells fashioned by other people, hells that are legacies from the long human past, while current society is manufacturing new and more gruesome ones. Jean-Paul Sartre has a character saying, "Hell is other people,"[1] while another writer has one bemoaning, "Myself am hell."[2] Unredeemed human life *is* hell.

We may debate about eschatological hell; existential hells are omnipresent and self-evident. As for those who say that a good God would not create a hell, God need only allow us to do it.

These are generalities about hells, but those suffering from them are not vague, faceless entities. They are the people all around us whose lives are being blighted and who need the assurance of a loving God at work in the universe. They are broken and the candidates for brokenness.

What are these hells? They are the despair of the alcoholic and other drug addicts and the agonies of their families. They are the desperation of the deprivation of those for whom "hope, unborn, had died." They are the loneliness of those for whom nobody cares. Hells are the maddening drive of ambition that permits no peace. They are the scourge of those who, brutalized as children, are driven by some demon to bru-

---

[1]In his 1947 play *No Exit*.
[2]John Milton, *Paradise Lost*.

talize their own. They are the oppression of those living with guilt, not knowing that it is a burden that they need not bear. They are the dread of children going to school daily in fear. The hells are—you name them!

God's wise providence gave humanity some built-in psychological adjustments to protect the nerves of those, like medical people, who constantly face suffering and death. Unfortunately, that same protection can inure us against the traumatic scenes all around us.

Transmitters of the love of God, we need the opposite of the inuring process: we need a sensitizing process that opens us up to those around us in sympathetic, empathetic responses. Paul admonishes us to "weep with those who weep" (Rom. 12:15).

Tears flow unsummoned, as Tennyson wrote:

> Tears, idle tears, I know not what they mean,
> Tears from the depth of some divine despair
> Rise in the heart, and gather to the eyes.
>   (Alfred, Lord Tennyson,
>   *The Princess*)

Jeremiah was agonizing over the nation when he cried: "O that my head were a spring of water, and my eyes a fountain of tears, so that I might weep day and night" (Jer. 9:1).

And in Lamentations 2:18: "Cry aloud to the Lord! . . . Let tears stream down like a torrent. . . . Give yourself no rest, your eyes no respite!"

Seeing the suffering of humanity, fired by the love God breathed into us and with faith in God's power to deal with those hells, we cannot be silent.

Our charge is not only to aid people in their hells, but to help them to avoid them down the road. Christ in life today can forestall drifting toward tomorrow's traumas. As life-sustaining, health-giving ways of living prevent illness, so living life God's way makes for heavens—not hells. The gospel is good news to the deprived, the lonely, the bruised and beaten, the guilty, to those who are seeking answers to life's questions where there are no answers. It is the simple faith of a child's "Jesus loves me, this I know" applied to life's most profound problems.

In the face of this, can we keep silent?

We must, however, ask ourselves, "Is it adequate to offer Christ for the hells of people and leave them unaided in conditions that foment their hells?" Is it not incumbent on the messenger to seek to give evidence that God cares for those whose hells are "other people"—that is, those whose hells are the creation of remediable socioeconomic-political conditions? James (James 2:14–17) and Jesus (Matt. 25:31–46) stressed the obligation to provide food and clothing, but that leaves them in the socioeconomic traps that create their unfortunate condition. God, who did not create a world for it to be millions of pits of hell, wants the good news to be acted out on the stage of history, as servants of the divine tackle the creators and creations of hell.

God would not have the church pray, "Thy will be done on earth," only to be excused from the struggle for a social and economic order that facilitates God's will in action.

Thus the love that Christ came to reintroduce into God's rebellious world was a love that would be salvation for individuals. It was a love to restore the integrity of human society. Jesus emphasized that God loved *the world* and would restore its true nature. Individuals are the transmitters.

An anecdote dramatizes this. Two men had worked together for years. Joe went to church every Sunday, Harvey not at all. One Monday morning, Harvey said, "Joe, I went to church yesterday," whereupon Joe responded excitedly, "Harve, I'm sure glad to hear that."

Harvey continued, "The preacher said some things that bothered me. He talked about the wonderful things that Christ does for those who accept him, and the great losses to those who do not. Do you believe that, Joe?"

Joe replied, "Sure, that's what it's all about."

Harvey burst out passionately, "No, Joe, you don't believe that."

Joe bristled. "Yes, I do believe that!"

Harvey shook his head sadly, saying, "No, Joe, you couldn't really believe that and work side by side with me all these years and never say a word about it. No, Joe, you don't believe it."

This story raises an unavoidable question. Can we experience the forgiving, healing, supporting love of God and remain mute about it? Harvey asks us, "Do you really believe what you say that you believe?"

Compulsion for evangelism is the drive from the impact of what Christ means in our lives and an awareness of the brokenness of individual lives and of human society. That compulsion is a surge of divine love to and through us.

Every proper motivation is shadowed by one or more counterfeit ones, and evangelism is no exception. The long, damaging decline in church membership sparks an intense concern with institutional health as measured by membership statistics. The result is a focus on "church growth."

Church growth is not to be scorned. Jesus' command to preach, teach, and baptize is a mandate to reach people for his church. He came for humanity, and there is undeniable failure when we do not let the Holy Spirit use us so that persons find their way to Christ and the church. Christ spoke of building his church (Matt. 16:18). Proper church growth is building Christ's church. But God did not so love the church that God gave his Son. God loved the world and brought the church into being as a means to serve God's people. We have seen earlier how a church membership recruitment program actually weakened the church.

One's goals determine one's techniques and strategies. If the goal is institutional preservation, techniques will focus on the institution. Comparison may be made to a hospital board, which is charged with the direction of the institution. It is not unknown for such a board to be so enamored of the image of the institution that decisions are made that do not keep the patient in focus. Purchase of exotic equipment and concentration on superspecialists have been known to cripple hospitals at their real point of service. Such concentration has sometimes placed them in financial straits so that emergency wards have had to be closed, curtailing service to those who cannot pay the going fees; the number of interns has been greatly reduced, thus reducing front-line medical service. Service to sick and hurting people has been a casualty of institutional hubris.

In the same manner, the church's fixation on church growth may easily blur the reasons for the church's existence. The church becomes the church's mission. The people whom God loves slip out of focus. Jesus' warning, "For those who want to save their life will lose it, and those who lose their life for my sake will find it" (Matt. 16:25), is true of institutions as well as of individuals.

Another fixation is on new church development as the panacea for statistical shortages. Developing new churches is important, in order that the church may be where the people are. But when creating new churches becomes the church's strategy as the cure for falling membership, it is set to be a failed strategy. If these new churches share the ailments that are making old ones ineffective, they are no cure for the church's illness.

Improving church membership by starting new churches can very well cover up the spiritual failings that have led to declining membership. The institution's health may seem to improve as measured by membership figures. But if hundreds of older churches are left languishing in apathy about their mission in *their* communities, the new churches will be merely mouth-to-mouth resuscitation while the patient continues the slide toward death.

As I travel around I see the Walton concern busily establishing new Wal-Marts and Mr. Sam's warehouse shopping. At the same time, I notice that every store I visit is a going concern, with its staff earnestly seeking to carry out the store's mission in that place. The leadership has not allowed the development of new units to spare them from making every established unit effective and efficient.

Unless the church's new-church development strategy is matched by opening up existing churches to the power of the Holy Spirit to make them and their members effective witnesses, dynamic conduits of the love of God, the future of the church will be at stake.

All that has been said in this chapter merely deals with how the love that compelled God to intervene in the human tragedy, can and should reverberate through the life of the church and the lives of God's people.

Waiting to board a bus at Madison, Wisconsin, en route to some evangelistic workshop, I noticed a package ready to be loaded. Printed on it was the following: HUMAN BLOOD, DO NOT DELAY. This was saying that somewhere out there were patients in a hospital needing that blood, and it should not be shoved into the dark recesses of the luggage compartment to ride up and down the highway. This said something to me about love compelling evangelism.

Jesus had to go through Samaria. So do we.

3

EVANGELISM IS GOING OUT OF THE WAY

As already noted, travel through Samaria was not the normal route for Jews. They had an intense contempt for the Samaritans, growing out of some unfortunate history. A brutal history of invasion, captivity, and occupation had ruptured the unity of the chosen people.

In 722 B.C., Sargon, King of Assyria, captured the area that was later known as Samaria, and took most of the people as captives to Assyria. Some of those left behind intermarried with captives imported from Babylon, Syria, and other places. Later, returning captives were shocked at this miscegenation that sullied the purity of the chosen people. For centuries now they had scorned this "mongrel" people.

To make matters worse, during the intervening centuries the Samaritans had made alterations in religious practices that further enraged the Jews. They accepted only the Torah as scripture, and had built a temple on Mount Gerizim, which rivaled the Temple on Mount Zion at Jerusalem. Those rival temples were the background of a question the Samaritan woman at the well asked about where worship should take place.

By Jesus' day this racial and religious animosity was so intense that asking for the courtesy of a drink of water was unexpected—this in a culture where hospitality to a stranger was almost a religious ritual. Jews wanted no contact with Samaritans, even in transit.

This might well have been the first time that the disciples had traveled this route, and from the glimpses we get of their very humanness, they probably grumbled every step of the way.

So Jesus was going out of his way—not geographically, but in departing from custom. Evangelism is going out of one's way. Going out of the way should often demand going physically out of the way, but very often may be just a change of custom, such as a different conversation with a friend at the farm implement store or during a lunch break on the job.

This cultural detour must be seen in the context of Jesus' mission. In John, chapter 3, the writer quotes Jesus as telling Nicodemus that God loved the world so much that God sent Jesus for the world's salvation. This detour, in spite of the restrictive things Jesus said about his mission (Matt. 10:5–6, e.g.), was just part of his cosmic detour, as we have noted more fully in chapter 2, "Acting under Compulsion of Love."

Dragging his unwilling disciples through Samaria may well have been part of Jesus' training for them. In the early postresurrection days, they were groping to find the scope of their mission. Peter would hardly have been prepared to accept the request of a Roman centurion to visit the centurion's home, so God gave him an object lesson. In a dream he saw a vision of animals, and he was instructed to kill something and eat. When he protested that he did not eat anything that was unclean, he was told not to call unclean what God had made clean (Acts 10:15). The "mission to Samaria" may well have been in preparation.

Evangelism is an endless chain reaction of going out of the way. Evangelists are people whom God has met on the divine detour. Their gratitude and enthusiasm send them on their own detours.

This has broad implications. It has implications for the church as a body. It has implications for individual Christians. It mandates going out of the way for the individual and the institution.

Basic Organization for Evangelism

The Spirit is the source of power, but like other power, it works through machinery—a basic organizational structure.

Congregations of every denomination have some body—deacons, elders, wardens—who have the human responsibility for guiding the work of the church. In most churches that structure breaks down into supporting committees. Even in small churches, if they are carrying out a full range of ministries, the work is too broad and varied for a normal-sized board to adequately manage. Despite all the joking about committees, this does call for some committee structure.

Evangelism deserves a committee with undivided attention. Many churches make it part of "outreach," but outreach can have so many responsibilities that it is not easy to give evangelism the attention that its priority status merits. If evangelism is the church's number one priority, it should report directly to the governing body. The chair may, or in many cases must, be a member of the ruling board. However, the membership should involve people from the congregation who are known to have the interest, commitment, knowledge, and spirit to lead the work of evangelistic outreach.

This sweeping mandate for committee structure must be qualified in the case of very small churches. It may well be advisable to use individual church leaders to carry the responsibility, and judgment has to be made whether the person should be a member of the governing board or not. In churches where women are not normally elected to the board, there are certainly some instances in which a dynamic woman should have that leadership. But, as with a committee, the lead person is not charged to do all the *work*. Various members should be asked to make telephone calls, visits, and otherwise lend their contacts and influence to the outreach.

We should point out that the number of members in "small churches" may vary widely, so leaders should not jump too readily to the idea that some committee structure is not for them.

The assignment of the committee is not to *do* the work of evangelism, but to guide and stimulate it while also participating as individuals. Evangelism is the work of the entire people of God. The committee may have subcommittees if the field of service is broad enough.

It is an ongoing responsibility, not a seasonal or occasional one. Educating the congregation and every organization to their responsibilities and opportunities is a function of the committee.

The Church Going out of Its Way—through Its Members

In seminars and workshops on evangelism, the first reply to my question as to how we can reach our public has almost always suggested some form of commercial advertising. This response indicates a lack of sensitivity as to what the church is offering. It is not something inanimate, like a bar of soap or a lawnmower. It is not something impersonal like a rug cleaning service. It is seeking to touch the deepest throbs of human life, and it is done in interpersonal relationships. For that work the church has the ideal resource—itself and its membership.

Seventy or so years ago, a Communist leader boasted that if he had the structure of the Christian church, with cells on every corner and millions of volunteer members, he would convert the world to communism in a generation. Having this coveted structure and personnel, why has the church not made that kind of advance? Why, indeed, is much of it, instead, in a seemingly interminable decline?

The reasons are many and varied, but a major one is that the church has never learned to use its primary asset—its membership. Stated obversely, the church membership has never grasped and committed itself to the role that is the natural outgrowth of its supposed faith. A church with a hundred members has a hundred people fanning out across the community, each with dozens, scores, some with hundreds of contacts, and between them immeasurable influence. Circulating through the community with an enthusiasm about the message of divine love, they have a terrific potential and should be a dynamic force.

Physicists say that there are no two snowflakes alike. Looking one day from my Omaha window at tons of them, I wondered how anybody knew. But as I mused on the subject, it occurred to me that in the masses of humanity, every individual is absolutely unique. Husband and wife may have exactly the same circle of friends and acquaintances, but their relationships and influence are not the same. Every individual has once-in-a-lifetime contacts and influences. There are no clones in God's economy. To realize that uniqueness is a thrilling thought. But there is a concomitant chilling thought: If one's contacts and influences are uniquely one's own, then only that person can use them; if that person fails to do so, they are eternally wasted. God may have some plan B to accomplish what God expected of that unique person, but then God may not. And the description of the final judgment looms threateningly (Matt. 25:31–46).

Jesus' parable of the last judgment recounts the rejection of those who failed to minister to physical human needs. As serious as that failure is for human life, it in no way approximates the failure to share the bread, water of life, and ministry with those imprisoned by sin. This is a message to the church, the significance of which it must grasp for itself and help every Christian to grasp.

The psalmist's cry, "What shall *I* return to the LORD for all his bounty to *me*?" (Ps. 116:12, italics added), dramatizes the personal nature of our relationship with God, out of which we speak to others.

The evidence is that this tremendous asset is largely squandered. People who are vocal about all sorts of things, including trivialities, are often hopelessly mute about what should be the most important thing in their lives. Their rationalizations are legendary and often absurd.

Inviting People to Church

Many Christians find themselves unable to talk easily about their faith. While the church must not be content to leave its members unable to talk about Christ and what their faith means to them, developing that power will take time and patient cultivation. Meanwhile, there is something that anyone can do. That bare minimum is to invite family, friends, acquaintances, and even strangers to join in the worship of the church. And beyond the invitation, one might consider bringing them and making them feel at home as one escorts them to the pew.

Experience shows that there is a strange reticence to perform even this minimal role in evangelism. The pastor and the evangelism committee may have to work tirelessly to develop this lay ministry. They should be prepared to learn that pushing a stalled car up a hill is no harder than getting most church members in nongrowing churches to invite people in their own families, blocks, places of employment, or social circles to church.

On occasion it has helped to name the first Sunday of the month as "visitors' Sunday." The only reason for designating the first Sunday is that it is more easily identifiable. It must then be carefully and consistently promoted. Some members begin to invite their non-church-related friends for the first Sunday, and after a while forget which Sunday is visitors' Sunday and it becomes a practice. It becomes contagious, and the church has the potential growing edge of a constant flow of visitors.

Perhaps inviting people to worship seems just too trivial. One is reminded of the story of Naaman, an officer in the Syrian army who had contracted leprosy (2 Kings 5:1–19). Learning from his wife's Israelite slave maid of a prophet in Israel who might cure him, he traveled to meet Elisha. Told by Elisha to go and bathe in the Jordan River, he flew into a rage, saying that the rivers of Damascus, flowing down from Mount Hermon, were vastly superior to that miserable little Jordan, so why should he bathe in it? A servant counseled him: "If the prophet had told you to do something difficult, would you not have done it?" Relenting, he obeyed and was healed. Maybe inviting someone to church seems just too insignificant.

What, really, can be its value?

Isaiah's conversion, discussed earlier, illustrates the importance of being in the worship experience. This was not Isaiah's first time at church. Why, this day, did this tremendous experience occur? We can only surmise, but one theory is that "the year King Uzziah died"—the common kind of dating phrase—was expressing not a time relationship but a causative one. Did Uzziah's death leave Isaiah bereft, so that he was open to a revelation from God in a way that he had never been before?

There is no way of knowing how and when the Spirit "blows where it chooses" (John 3:8). Great joy or sorrow, aching emptiness, fear and uncertainty—all sorts of human states of mind and spirit may be at work at some particular time, making someone open to hear God's voice and message. Or there may have been a cumulative impact from earlier worship experiences that have come to fruition. Ours is not to know; ours is to speak for God and give the Holy Spirit a chance.

Someone may despair of anything happening because of personally finding the worship to be routine. But what is to the old hand an "old, old story" may be fresh good news to the person one has invited to worship on any particular Sunday.

There are other reasons for patience. Getting people into the worship experience exposes them to the teaching of the Word of God. They may have little background for understanding what they are hearing and experiencing. With fifteen- to thirty-minute sermons on different subjects, if they are not already biblically literate, it may take some time for the message of the gospel to become clear. The host can help the learner to understand.

But worship—true worship—is more than an intellectual experience. It touches the deep springs of human emotions—the loves, the hates, the guilts, hopes, and dreams. In these worship experiences, life begins to make sense as spiritual journeys are made.

Many give up too easily. In our hurry-up culture we easily grow impatient if results do not show quickly. With instant coffee, instant cereals, flowers, and trees there today that were not there yesterday, we lose the feel of long and careful cultivation. The tree may have been transplanted in a day, but it took years for someone to grow it.

After a friend drops in occasionally and nothing happens, we tend to give up, when we should be graciously, not naggingly, persistent. I know a congregation that went into spiritual ecstasy when an elderly lady who had been in its prayer and visitation focus for seven years responded to the Sunday morning invitation to discipleship.

It is strange that Christians who give so that others might cross the seas to touch lives with the gospel think it improper to cross the street to do the same. Some African friends asked me why Christians in this country are so concerned about bringing the gospel to Africa and so indifferent to carrying it to their neighbors.

Some completely inanimate things may be part of our appeal. At nearby intersections, signs may point the way to the church. Arriving, the visitor sees a neat, attractive building and grounds.

Our responsibility does not end, however, with getting the person there. As we go out of our way to expose people to God's message in worship, it is important that we provide the most conducive setting. This is a total church responsibility.

The ushers or greeters see that the first impression inside the building is warm and friendly.

Persons in the pews are cordial, sharing or even surrendering a hymnal, assisting with something unfamiliar in the service.

The music is inspiring and uplifting. If there is a good choir, all the better, but vigorous congregational singing is also uplifting. Familiar hymns, well sung, may awaken memories in the visitor's mind of childhood and youth family worship experiences.

The preacher may not be a master of homiletics, but the sermon is scripturally sound and relevant to life, and has the ring of sincerity.

The congregation is friendly after the service. If there is a "fellowship time," the fellowship makes sure to include the visitor. Otherwise the visitor may set the cup down and slip unobtrusively out—perhaps forever.

Every member, young and older, can be part of this evangelistic process.

The Church Going out of Its Way—as an Organization

Most churches have visible and identifiable structures in the community. Others, whose architecture may not proclaim them as churches, generally have signs to indicate that they are, as well as what branch of the church they represent. The building declares, "The church is here." Why don't they come?

In our community, construction began on what was obviously to be some commercial establishment. Eventually a sign proclaimed that it would be a new unit of a popular grocery chain. For months we saw it rise and take shape, but when it was ready for business the owners did not depend on our long observation of it to turn us into customers. They erected a GRAND OPENING sign. They advertised in newspapers. They got flyers into every mailbox, telling us about the great bargains available, with many items marked below cost. They wanted us there.

By contrast, we have lived for nineteen years about two hundred yards from a church. Not once has anybody come to our door or even dropped an invitation in our mailbox. There is a bulletin board on church property that invites us to come, but that is the limit of their seeking us. It is not a Presbyterian church, but it is more typical than we would like to admit.

Jesus said that "the children of this age are more shrewd in dealing with their own generation than are the children of light" (Luke 16:8). Commercial ventures spare no effort to make contact with potential customers. They study the market, analyze the needs and desire of potential customers, inform them of what they have, and seek to get them to come into their facility to buy their products. Other types of businesses seek to get their representatives into the homes or offices of those with whom they seek to do business. They are convinced, or at least seek to convince the prospective customer, that they have something available that the person needs or desires. They even seek to create an artificial sense of need, convincing prospects that they "just can't get along without it."

The grocery store had things that we knew we needed. There were some items that we needed, but would not have thought of. A favorite sales technique is to scatter spices throughout the store, so that the eye falls on them and we are reminded that we are out of one or have a new recipe that calls for a spice that we have not needed heretofore. We had the need, but the awareness had to be stimulated. People may or may not be aware of their spiritual needs. They may need to be reminded or stimulated to action.

There are, of course, limitations to the validity of the analogy of the wisdom of the commercial world. The admonition of Jesus about being as wise as the children of this world was given in a parable about a manager who had mismanaged his employer's assets. About to be apprehended, he did some hasty discounting of debts in order to make friends for his dismal future. The employer complimented him for his shrewdness, and Jesus pointed to his shrewdness, not his chicanery, as an example (Luke 16:1–9).

The church and its members are surrounded by people who are desperately in need of what Christ offers in the gospel and through the church. The potential "customers" are there; the needs are there; the church does not have to create artificial desires. Like the merchant, we do need to make some potential customers aware of their needs and the availability of resources to meet their needs.

The Head of the church knows those needs, and the whole thrust of Christ's mission is to meet those needs at the deepest level. Surrounded by broken lives and lives that are candidates for brokenness, one has to wonder why churches that are entrusted with a message for healing are not sharing it eagerly and widely, why churches with the message of joy and victory are not excitedly telling about it. If the church is convinced that the bread of life is available for the spiritually hungry, a hunger that cannot be satisfied with junk foods; that the water of life is available for the spiritually thirsty, a thirst that cannot be slaked by spiritual colas; that there is healing for spiritual illness—it should be ranging far and wide out of its way to contact those people. The late D. T. Niles described evangelism as one beggar telling another where he had found some bread.

The church should seek to know its market—the needs of humanity. This demands study of human nature, but from God's point of view. John (chap. 2:23–25) says that Jesus "knew all people and needed no one to testify about anyone; for he himself knew what was in everyone" and "understood human nature" (Phillips). Jesus understood human nature, so he was able to cut through the superficial when a man asked him to be a court referee in settling an estate (Luke 12:13–21). He addressed the man's real need—not the wealth he coveted, but to be relieved of covetousness.

It is knowing desires at a deeper level than the expressed desires of persons, knowing needs as the physician knows the patient's needs. It is knowing that underneath the craving for colas and junk foods are deep, God-created thirsts and hungers that long for satisfaction.

Isaiah sounds the call to abundant life:

> Ho, everyone who thirsts,
> come to the waters;
> and you that have no money,
>   come, buy and eat!
> Come, buy wine and milk
>   without money and without price.
> Why do you spend your money for that which is not bread,
>   and your labor for that which does not satisfy?
> Listen carefully to me, and eat what is good,
>   and delight yourselves in rich food.
> Incline your ear, and come to me;
>   listen, so that you may live.
>
> (Isa. 55:1–3)

Commerce, even when it knows its market, may cater to real, perceived, or imaginary needs, with no distinction. To evaluate desires is not its concern, only to at least temporarily satisfy them. For thirst it may offer colas and the like, artificial thirst quenchers. The needs and desires of natural hunger may be met with solid, nutritious food or with junk foods, with high concentrations of fats, sugars, cholesterol, or other elements, pernicious in their volume. Madison Avenue is under no compulsion to analyze the true nature of hunger.

The church's market analysis differs from that of the commercial world. The true church does not seek to magnify or exploit the super-ficial desires of its public, nor does its marketing strategy pander to them, although some elements of the church do just that. The most glar-ing examples are some of the electronic "ministries." These are, how-ever, only the most successful, and thus the best known. Many local pulpits give the people "what they want," a travesty on the gospel.

The manufacturers and purveyors of goods have used the realities of science and the physical world to develop those things which they seek to sell. Evangelism deals just as much with the realities of how the world is created. Based on the revelation from God, known through scripture and human searching, the church has something to offer that conforms to the realities of God's created world. As God provided for meeting the needs of physical hunger, thirst, tiredness, illness, and bro-kenness, so God provides the means to meet those same needs of the spirit. Evangelism is trying to know the needs, to know God's re-sources, and to connect them in health-giving, life- and soul-saving, and social-healing ways.

Knowing its market means that the church needs to know what the social sciences have learned about human nature. It needs to know what the psychologists know. It needs to know the contemporary so-cial context and its implications for human life. Insofar as these sciences have learned the truth, it is God's truth, but their grasp of truth must always be seen through the lens of the gospel.

The wider church enters here. Seminaries, continuing education programs, curriculum writers, and independent theologians have the responsibility to do research and interpret for the people in the field the intricacies of knowledge and the implications for their ministry.

Knowing its market, that is, with knowledge of the customer and knowledge of what the gospel has to offer, the church devises strate-gies to make contact with potential customers. These strategies must be based on the nature, mission, and resources of the church. Otherwise it may be guilty of false advertising—with deleterious results.

Reference was made earlier to newspaper advertising. We must rec-ognize that people who turn to the religious page are by that very act identified as "warm prospects." They may be new people in town, searching for a church of their denomination, or visitors in the area looking for an interesting place to worship. But seldom will they be the persons most in need of the creative outreach of the church. This is not to say that the "To whom it may concern" approach has no validity; it is to say that it hardly merits being the first thought to come to mind in seeking to develop outreach to the unchurched.

The supermarket in our earlier example used the newspaper, but its use of the "Occupant" technique was certainly even more effective. This offers some improvement over the "To whom it may concern" approach for the church. The person approached does not have to go to the right place in the newspaper to get the message. An "Occupant" mailing or hand-delivered leaflet may be thrown away without a glance, or may, with the volume of junk mail received, be resented. But it at least reaches the potential customer. Like other advertising, it has its limitations.

Current "junk mail" practices make it technically easy to reach people in a selected area with advertising. This kind of contact needs to be studied in urban communities, where apartment dwellers may be as inaccessible as the ancient cliff dwellers who climbed up their ropes and pulled the ropes up after them. Any communication would need to be eye-catching in design and wording. To be effective it must be of professional quality and done with a high degree of sophistication. It must give the "feel" of the church and its ministries. And it must be based on some understanding of the nature of the people it is intended to reach. At best it is a random shot, but if Paul could be "all things to all people, that I might by all means save some" (1 Cor. 9:22), a church with the financial and human resources to skillfully reach out to these modern cliff dwellers might find the effort blessed by the Spirit.

More personalized efforts to contact people are based on knowing who the people are. "Occupant" must change to "Mrs.," "Ms.," "Mr.," "Mr. and Mrs.," or "Mr. and Mrs. . . . and family." Moving to this level demands organized, overt, even aggressive action on the part of the church family. It calls for systematically learning who is in the community.

Alert and concerned members contribute information about nonchurched relatives, friends, and colleagues, and the church follows up. It would seem that this information would flow easily, but experience shows that the leadership will probably have to work patiently to motivate members to give such information. Cards may be in the pew racks, but oral reminders will have to be made.

The alert church seizes on the enthusiasm of new members, who become new points of contact in the community. With the motivation that inspired them to respond, they are likely to be ready to share their enthusiasm. Beginning this way, then, may well assure a continuing flow of information.

A small church in the small town or rural area has a distinct advantage, since people generally know one another. But that advantage becomes a handicap if the leadership assumes that no thought or planning is needed to see that persons are not overlooked. The church needs to be alert and give attention to those familiar people. Familiarity may breed ignorance.

Farmer Brown may have been seen going about his chores so many Sunday mornings that he has become simply part of the scenery.

Persons of different social and economic strata may have become invisible.

Hospital staff and others whose work takes Sunday mornings can very easily be forgotten.

Every church, however small and face-to-face a community it may serve, should constantly be looking to see who is out there.

A place to look for people, regardless of the size of church and community, is in the families of church members. Failing to respond over years (or maybe having been ignored all the time), some may have dropped out of mind, if not out of sight. Ministering to one's own family may be the most awkward responsibility, but it is not just the mission of the blood family. The family should enlist the help of the church.

All identifiable persons who claim no relationship to Christ and/or the church should be on the church's records, in its work plans, and in its prayers.

Neighborhood Canvass

Neighborhood canvass work is the most systematic way of gathering information and making initial contacts. It replaces the haphazard, hit-or-miss procedure in locating people. It has difficulties, but carrying out a mission that led its originator to a cross, and which (according to tradition) led ten of the original Twelve to their own martyr deaths, does not apologize for giving difficult tasks to modern-day disciples. Jesus prepared his disciples for rebuffs and rejections, and that includes us.

God, who created a world of order, is not averse to using that order in the divine redemption effort. The work of salvation is the work of the Holy Spirit, but the Spirit uses plans, equipment, and training processes and has updated to the computer, and even the camcorder and VCR can be tools of the Spirit.

Doing effective canvass work demands careful planning, organization, execution, and follow-up. It needs to be assigned to a special committee of people chosen because they have the interest, drive, and organizational skills to plan and execute an efficient operation that should leave the congregation more unified and enthusiastic.

A canvass demands its own set of materials, carefully designed to secure the needed information with minimum risks of awkward, embarrassing situations. It will probably be necessary for the committee to design and produce them.

The structure for organizing and leading a canvass may be as simple or complex as the size of the church and community demands. Possibilities range from a three-person committee in a small church to a large one with subcommittees in larger situations. But the canvass must be in the hands of a special group.

In organizing the work, the leaders should look for persons in the congregation (or they may enlist friends) whose work gives them some particularly helpful skills.

> A postal worker may be helpful in plotting the area.
>
> A social worker may counsel about the types of family situations that may be met, and could help design the information-gathering tool.
>
> A law enforcement person may counsel about safety issues.
>
> Somebody with the necessary craft skills might produce identification badges.
>
> A scout troop might distribute leaflets to homes prior to the canvass to smooth the way for canvassers.

The search may uncover people who would be ecstatic to know that they could be useful in an evangelism effort.

Not everyone will be selected for the actual canvassing work, but alert use of various skills can make it a real all-congregation project.

The committee should take ample time to organize thoroughly.

Possible Format for Organizing a Canvass

I. Developing canvass materials

  A. Information to be sought

    1. Names and sex of people in the home. The old assumption of a nuclear family is long passé. The information tool must be designed to secure the desired information with minimal risk of embarrassment to either the worker or the person visited. It may be wise to use a single-person card in addition to or instead of a family-type card. Single people, with or without children, husbands, wives, his children, her children, their children, and homosexual couples are all possibilities.

    2. Ages and sex of children

    3. Present *active* church membership, if any, and in what town. The term "active" should be stressed to lessen the likelihood of being misled by out-of-date information.

  B. Materials to leave

    1. Good information brochure or sheet about the church. This may be as elaborate or as simple as the circumstances warrant. It should include information about the church's ministries and services, pastor's name, church address, and telephone number. With discretion, canvassers may leave their names and telephone numbers.

  C. Materials for filing

    1. The original canvass card

    2. A work sheet or computer record showing the canvass information, designed to carry a running record of all follow-up and response, such as church attendance, participation in activities, or services rendered by church or pastor

II. Organizing the canvass

  A. Deciding whether to work singly or in pairs

  B. Determining the area to be covered

    1. Avoiding overextending that would delay follow-up

    2. Beginning with the immediate neighborhood, except for

downtown churches and rural areas, whose demography will dictate their approach

3. Using a city directory—with this, addresses can be plotted and names noted, keeping in mind that occupancy may have changed.
4. Giving advance notice of visitation by:
    (a) fliers attached to mailboxes or left in doors
    (b) announcement in community newspapers
    (c) radio or television public service notices

III. Selecting canvassers
   A. Characteristics needed
      1. Maturity (emotional and psychological)
      2. Tact
      3. Friendliness
      4. Ability and knowledge to answer questions about Christianity and the church, although it should be stressed that this call should be limited as far as possible to gathering information

      (Do not ask for volunteers.)
   B. Training canvassers
      1. Explaining materials
      2. Discussing "how to":
         (a) open the conversation
         (b) explain the reason for the visit
         (c) secure the information
         (d) deal with difficult situations
         (e) gracefully end the visit
      3. Using VCR for role-playing instruction beforehand

IV. Follow-up
   A. Receiving, digesting, and organizing the data
   B. Being alert for any persons visited who come to worship
   C. Mailing acknowledgments to those being put in records
   D. Beginning the process of cultivation of those who indicate no involvement with Christianity or not being related to a local church
   E. Mailing the canvass cards to the churches where some claimed membership, as an ecumenical courtesy

These are general guidelines from experiences with canvass work in a major city. Any particular church, with its knowledge of itself, the creativity of its members, and knowledge of its community can tailor-make its canvass.

Small town and rural churches would, of necessity, adjust the general principles given here.

All urban churches would eventually reach out to more remote areas, but downtown churches might begin with areas where their members live.

The essentials for successful canvass work are:

1. Careful planning
2. Careful preparation of materials
3. Careful selection of canvassers
4. Careful recording of data
5. Follow-up without fail
6. All of these done prayerfully

There are results from neighborhood canvass work that are not recorded and can never be measured. They are the impact on neighbors of the church's reaching out to them. An often reported statement has been, "I have lived here for X number of years, and this is the first time that any Protestant or Catholic church has ever come to my door." The visitation itself is witness—often effective witness.

Other Means of Primary Contact

Concern, alertness, and imagination are the keys, and the means of reaching out are legion.

Many churches have scouts, 4-H clubs, vacation church schools, and recreational programs that involve children and youth whose families are not related to the church. A church should have a systematic back-trail to every such home. Churches should aggressively develop such community activities that reach beyond their constituency, both to better serve community needs and to be tentacles of outreach for evangelism. The too-often-heard complaint that children and youth activities "mess up the building" stands opposed to Jesus' mandate: "Let the little children come to me" (Mark 10:14).

The church building itself is a potential evangelistic asset. Making it available to community groups whose programs are uplifting shows a spirit of neighborliness and cooperation that can make friends. In addition, making their way to the church building repeatedly may encourage people to make their way there for worship. Regular trips will make some feel at home for whom the church would otherwise be a strange place.

Nearby military bases or installations offer special challenges and opportunities to communities. The weak-commitment church may be dissuaded from outreach, because the transient nature of the population does not make for solid membership growth. But these personnel have special needs, and the chaplain is often too identified with the military brass to encourage their seeking confidential pastoral care. Churches in communities so impacted may be able to secure special funding to aid with such ministry, especially if done ecumenically.

In some communities it is possible to identify newcomers to the city or area of the city through utility connections.

There are an increasing number of church-serving firms who compile such lists according to zip codes and sell them to churches.

Information can often be had from the Welcome Wagon, and its representatives should have information about your services.

Evangelism is the work of the whole church. The pastor has a dual role: One is leading the work of the church, and evangelism is a major element of the witness to God's love. The pastor also has a personal role. The pastoral snowflake is as unique as the layperson's, and the pastor witnesses as a person, not just professionally.

The pastor has some relationships that give special opportunities. Often through weddings and funerals the pastor meets new people. While not intruding on those events, and certainly not transgressing on grief, such situations give the pastor opportunities to show love, concern, and understanding that are witness in their own right. Information can be garnered that can be followed up at some more appropriate time. If "I am the resurrection and the life" has meaning in terms of the deceased, it must have meaning for survivors.

Aside from contact with its potential market discussed earlier, other lessons can be learned from commerce. There are organizations that sponsor home parties for sales. Members may be encouraged to invite friends to their homes on Sunday evenings for conversation with the pastor about the Christian faith. They may come out of curiosity, out of genuine interest, or in some cases to vent their hostilities against the church. As people relax over refreshments, the sessions can be enjoyable and effective. And maybe the pastor will learn more than anyone in those open, soul-to-soul encounters. They can have good results.

These are but examples of the ways that churches can make contact with those who are not related to a faith or to a church, to people who have conscious or unconscious deep soul needs. It is all based on the faith that God would have the church be the human part of the delivery system of the good news that God so loved the world. . . .

We go out of our way to identify people who do not know that good news. We encourage them to come and worship. We make their visits warm, meaningful, and worshipful. We minister to them in whatever ways possible. So we have made a start on a journey which we will follow in later chapters.

4

EVANGELISM IS CROSSING BARRIERS

Jesus was showing his utter disregard for society's artificial barriers in having this conversation with the Samaritan woman. He did that in the first place just by being there. Jesus saw humanity as astronauts see this earth—as an unbroken entity, with nothing to show our petty little "fences." Much of the religious leaders' animosity toward him was rooted in his refusal to be fenced in or to be fenced away from people. Their concepts of God and religion separated them from people; Jesus' knowledge of the Father and of creation bound him to them. So this conversation, though it would have branded him as immoral, was just natural to Jesus.

Ms. Samaritan was not necessarily surprised that he broke the moral code by addressing her. The well area would have been the scene of prostitution at odd hours such as this, and men did start conversations at the well that they would never have engaged in in town. So she was not necessarily surprised that a Jew spoke to a Samaritan woman at the well—at high noon, anyway. But he was breaking a barrier raised by racial animosities.

It wasn't just her nationality as a Samaritan that threw up fences. In that society a man did not address a strange woman, even of his own people. Strike two against Jesus.

Even Samaritan men did not have social relations with Ms. Samaritan—not in public, at least. She was at the well at noon because the village ostracized her, and her being at the well at noon told Jesus: You don't talk to this kind of woman. He did. That kind of association was Jesus' pattern, as may be seen by the number of times he was criticized for eating and drinking with the wrong people (Matt. 9:10–13). He who came to save sinners was not about to be walled off from any particular variety by the customs and biases of other sinners. He knocked over that barrier.

Jews had strict rules about food, drink, and utensils. The earlier translation of the woman's response to his request—"Jews have no dealings with the Samaritans" (King James Version)—becomes a parenthetical observation in the New Revised Standard Version: "Jews do not share things in common with Samaritans." She was probably referring to the ban on using food vessels that were "unclean." Jesus ignored this too.

When Ms. Samaritan raised the issue of religious differences to divert the conversation, Jesus raised the conversation to a level at which there was no barrier.

One of the continuing and expanding results of sin is brokenness in the human family. Scripture says that there is one humanity. Creation says there is one humanity. Science says there is one humanity. Wherever I have traveled, among people of all sorts of physical, linguistic, and cultural differences, I have had one great consolation: in spite of all the differences, if I needed blood there would be someone in that place whose blood type would match mine!

But sin and selfishness have created multiple ruptures in the fabric of human society. We are separated by nationality, by race and clan, by social and economic classes, by religions, and even by cults and sects within religions. A friend with worldwide experience laments humanity's infinite capacity for separating itself.

The key to our faith is that God loved the world. We have earlier noted that the long development of creating a people into which Jesus was to come was a process of educating a crude, tribal people, who thought that God was their tribal deity, through long socio-moral-ethical refinement to the place that this seed of one world under God could germinate and thrive.

It was not easy for the early church, steeped in Jewish tradition, to accept the implications of what they said and believed—that God loved the *world*.

Barriers existed in the Christian fellowship from the beginning. In the euphoria of the resurrection and the hope of Christ's early return, a generous community of love and sharing was born. But even in this idyllic situation, the specter of ethnicity seems to have raised its ugly head. It was reported—and we can well believe—that the Grecian widows complained that they were being neglected in the daily distribution of food. Stephen and six others were called as deacons because of this discrimination (Acts 6:1–6).

We noted in the last chapter how God dealt with the Jewish barriers that lay deep in Peter's heart. He had his lesson in a vision as he called the things of God's creation unclean. Shortly afterward, messengers from Cornelius, a Roman centurion, arrived to ask Peter to come to his home in Caesarea. Realizing the meaning of his vision, Peter went, thus associating not only with a Gentile, but with a hated Roman. Peter was breaking barriers.

As Peter opened the gospel to them, Cornelius and his household were converted and filled with the Holy Spirit. Those with Peter raised no objection to their being baptized. They were baptized, and Peter and his colleagues remained for several days in this forbidden company (Acts 10:1–48).

But it was "barriers as usual" at the home church when this was reported, and there was a furor in Jerusalem. However, when Peter and his colleagues related what had happened, the church praised God (Acts 11:1–18).

The matter did not end there. Some persons came from Judea to raise the barrier of circumcision, saying that Gentiles must first become Jews before they could be Christians. After strong witness by Paul and Barnabas of the mighty things God had done among Gentiles, James, as head of the council, decreed that this barrier should not be maintained (Acts 15:1–35).

Elsewhere, the writer of the Letter of James decries class prejudices in the early church:

> My brothers and sisters, do you with your acts of favoritism really believe in our glorious Lord Jesus Christ? For if a person with gold rings and fine clothes comes into your assembly, and if a poor person in dirty clothes also comes in, and if you take notice of the one wearing the fine clothes and say, "Have a seat here, please," while to the one who is poor you say, "Stand there," or "Sit at my feet," have you not made distinctions among yourselves, and become judges with evil thoughts? (James 2:1–4)

These early examples of human-erected barriers presage a steady stream of rents in the seamless robe of the church through the subsequent centuries. Their nature, shape, and pattern have varied with cir-

cumstances, but they have always been present, and today their oc-
currence accelerates.

James was challenging the barrier of economic class. There are undeniable symptoms of classism in some of the older established denominations, and human nature being what it is, one would have to
believe that they exist in other denominations as well, though perhaps
in differing patterns.

In a 1975 *Study of Membership Trends,* the United Presbyterian
Church found some statistics that should have been disturbing. The ac-
companying figures show the comparative occupational, educational,
and income ratios between the church and the population in general.
There is no later study.

Ratios, UPC and General Population (1975)

OCCUPATIONAL
Professional and Technical

General Population	14.8%
United Presbyterian	19.0

Managers, Officials, Owners

General Population	11.4
United Presbyterian	53.0

Clerical

General Population	17.8
United Presbyterian	6.7

Sales

General Population	6.7
United Presbyterian	7.0

Crafts/Foremen/Labor

General Population	49.4
United Presbyterian	14.3

EDUCATIONAL
Less than High School

General Population	40.2
United Presbyterian	10.45

High School Only
    General Population   35.8
    United Presbyterian   23.8

Some College
    General Population   12.6
    United Presbyterian   24.8

College Graduate
    General Population   12.6
    United Presbyterian   41.1

INCOME
Under $5,000
    General Population   16.6
    United Presbyterian   4.1
$5,000 to $9,999
    General Population   27.1
    United Presbyterian   14.9
$10,000 to $14,999
    General Population   26.1
    United Presbyterian   23.8
$15,000 and Over
    General Population   30.3
    United Presbyterian   57.1%

Without doubt, some other churches would show similar profiles. This raises a serious question: What are the barriers that deter what we might call "working class" people from entering in strong numbers into the membership of some denominations? The fact that they don't is tragic, surmounted only by the tragedy that the church is largely unaware of it or, being aware, seems quite indifferent.

The Barrier of Worship

An explanation sometimes given is, "They don't appreciate our type of worship." Often said in self-laudation, it may be a self-condemnation. Its acceptance may be a manifestation of a kind of re-

**Occupations of Head of Household—
United Presbyterian and U.S. Population**

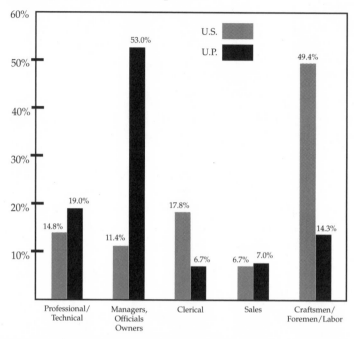

Source: *Presbyterian Panel* Background Questionnaire (January, 1973). U.S. Bureau of the Census, *General Population Characteristics, U.S. Summary,* U.S. Government Printing Office, Washington, D.C., 1972.

ligious elitism. It is true that not everybody responds to the same type of worship. But if Presbyterian worship and sermons turn off the masses, then Presbyterians must seek to learn why, and what they can do to change it.

In chapter 7, on deep spiritual truths, pains are taken to show how Jesus interpreted the gospel to the masses and how they received it gladly. The masses of his day had much less education than the masses who are not attracted to our churches, yet they were able to understand and grasp the gospel as he gave it.

We pride ourselves on the intellectual quality of our worship, and Christianity is truly a faith of thought and reason. However, this intellectual content is often exalted in opposition to emotional content. When we exalt intellectual quality, not for itself but in contrast to an

Educational Attainment—
United Presbyterian and U.S. Population

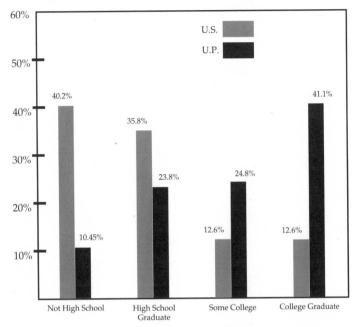

Source: *Presbyterian Panel* Background Questionnaire (January, 1973). U.S. Bureau of the Census, *Statistical Abstract of the United States, 1973* (94th edition), Washington, D.C., 1973.

emotional quality of worship, we may be exalting a weakness, not a strength. Repeatedly we find ourselves defining ourselves by contrast to others. In resisting the way some others work at evangelism, as we noted earlier, we risk locking ourselves into immobility. In the same manner, in rejecting what we consider the overemotionalism of some other styles of worship we may lock ourselves into a sterile intellectualism.

The minister looks out on a collection of serene faces on Sunday morning. But back of those calm faces is a sampling of the gamut of human experiences. People are bursting with joy and in the slough of depression. Some rejoice in their children and some are in despair for theirs. A couple had a squabble, rode to church in stolid silence, and are now sitting in the pew in close proximity, separated by a chasm. People

Family Income—
United Presbyterian and U.S. Population

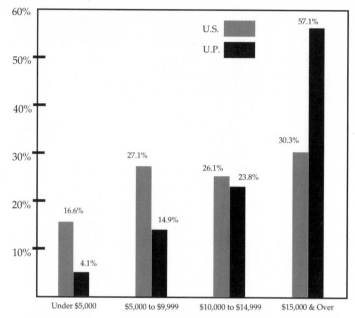

Source: *Presybterian Panel* Background Questionnaire (January, 1973). U.S. Bureau of the Census, *Statistical Abstract of the United States, 1973* (94th edition), Washington, D.C., 1973.

bring memories of sins of ambition, of greed, and of the flesh. They are jealous of the success of someone else or someone else's children. They are glowing with plans for a coming marriage or sick at heart about one that is disintegrating. They come with burdens of sin and guilt, with fears and discouragement. They come from happy homes and homes that are previews of hell. They are flushed with success and crushed by defeat. Many are silently crying for God's presence and guidance in their lives. And above all, they are needing love and the assurance of love, many not even realizing it. Like Isaiah, they may be open to the vision. They are human beings—Methodists, Pentecostals, Catholics, and Presbyterians at worship.

With this mosaic of human emotions in the pews, there is something questionable about a church where the only tears of joy or sorrow shed, the only visible or audible expressions of feelings, are at weddings and funerals. If the minister is being a pastor, not just an administrator, he or she is sharing in these lives as pastor and counselor. How can such a pastor preach without passion, or lead an emotion-free worship?

In such patterns we are worshiping as "hypocrites," not in the current sense of the word, but in the sense of its root in Greek theater, that of wearing masks. Instead of being a loving, supportive community, we are an assemblage of actresses and actors, in a weekly performance. We dare not let ourselves be known.

A growing number of churches have an informal time before or during the worship when people can speak openly of their joys, sorrows, and concerns. Despite all the danger of such a practice becoming just another *pro forma* ritual, it can be a step toward developing the caring community.

The psychological sciences tell us that, although the mind may set the direction, the will is powered greatly by the emotions. The mind may be the steering wheel, but the feelings are the motor and transmission. We have insisted that Christian love is not merely a good feeling toward someone, but we have noted that love is the driving force of the divine mission, the dynamic of the Christian life. Christian worship must reach deep down where the waves of passion surge—passion for good or for evil.

Jesus is recorded as weeping in two situations, and we are sure that his life was a constant outpouring of the depths of feeling. One of the recorded instances was in a personal situation, when he wept at the death of Lazarus (John 11:28–36). The other was for the society, as he wept over Jerusalem (Luke 19:41–44). He showed passion many times, including in the well incident, when he called the disciples to see the fields white with harvest.

The order of worship may be the same in two churches, even the selection of hymns and scripture. But the contagious enthusiasm of a hymn of praise, or the gentle feeling of a prayer hymn, will touch the wellsprings of lives in one congregation and be missing in the mere formality of another. The scripture may be read formally or with depth of feeling. The two sermons may be on the same lectionary text and with the same structure. One may be as unfeeling as a dull classroom lecture and the other touching the depths of many hearts.

It has been sometimes pathetic to see the hungry eagerness with which many pastors have seized each new worship aid or technique, eagerly hoping for some external nostrum to give life to worship. Often those who use the new worship aids most effectively are those who need them least. If our worship is stiff and devoid of feeling, then let us identify one barrier—an internal one.

There are occasional symptoms of the craving for more feeling in the worship of some denominations. One is the eagerness with which some people have seized on a type of music that may be characterized as cola music—light and frothy, bubbly in musical form and lyrics with the most trivial meaning. It represents a protest against the cold deadness that prevails in many churches.

Another cry for help is represented in the charismatic movement. It is a legitimate protest against the unfeeling character of much of the worship in a number of denominations. It is no accident that this feeling-laden movement has flourished in direct proportion to the formality and ritualistic character of much worship. Unfortunately, it has been difficult to blend into the life of many congregations. As some of its adherents practice it, it appears to be like the worship of some other denominations who claim that they have something superior, and this can be offensive. On the other hand, anything different offends many traditionalists, so that they reject the whole concept of the charismatic movement. But it is a legitimate cry from some worshipers for help.

Some hymnal revisions are exacerbating the condition. Traditional hymns with deep roots of meaning are judged not to be theologically correct enough. The cerebral has prevailed; the didactic has become dominant. While these efforts at improving hymnals have their value, there may be more need for "trade-offs," to give a balance.

As a young black minister, born and raised Presbyterian, trained in a Presbyterian seminary and pattern, I was aware that I was resisting some natural tendencies resulting from my exposure to worship and preaching in the black denominations. I was determined to be "Presbyterian." Then on one occasion I sat under the teaching of a young white Presbyterian minister with a Ph.D. degree, whose father, grandfather, and great-grandfather had been Presbyterian ministers, and whose family had been Presbyterian when my foreparents were slaves. He became emotionally involved in his message, his voice broke, and he wiped away a tear. I realized then that I could be true to my heritage and be a good Presbyterian too.

I do not have the answer to the unavoidable question—"If legitimate feelings are not adequately expressed in our worship, how does true emotion take its place in worship? How can those denominations with integrity allow the Holy Spirit to fire them in worship?" I can only make some too-superficial suggestions, suggestions that the pastor and selected leadership might seek to carry out.

1. Do not defensively reject the thought that the narrowness of the appeal of your church to the people all around you may say something to you about your worship.

2. Do not assume that your worship, probably ultimately rooted in worship a long time ago and in a different cultural situation, is necessarily the best worship form and mood for today.

3. Give serious thought and study to the worship pattern of your church.

4. Visit some churches that have different worship patterns and that are growing. Many of them have Sunday evening services, making it convenient to join in their worship. If one is accessible, include a leading African American church. Try to be objective, not rejecting everything because some aspects of the worship are unappealing to you. Worship with them several times.

5. Discuss your worship with congregational leadership and with members. Be prepared for total rejection of any thought of change.

6. Let the Holy Spirit, rather than habit or personal prejudice, guide you in your earnest evaluation of the nature of worship.

7. There are flourishing churches in your own denomination. If there are any in your area, worship with them and discuss with the pastors and members the nature of their worship.

Change does not mean taking over completely another pattern of worship. It may simply suggest some alterations in your own.

This is not to insist that what your church needs is change in worship. As will be seen in this book, there are numerous factors that militate for or against a growing church. But be sure that worship is not one of them.

The Barrier of Class

Other barriers that stand between many churches and the people around them are infiltrations of attitudes into the church from the secular society. The church functions within the context of society, so that it and its members live in two worlds, the social order and the kingdom of God. The church has always had to cope with pressures to conform to the society. Paul admonished the Roman Christians not to conform to society (Rom. 12:2). But social customs have their corrosive effects on the church's standards and quality of life. Society, then, has inevitably had its impact on evangelism as one dimension of the church's life.

The United Presbyterian statistics from 1975 show beyond doubt that that church was limited in its educational, economic, and employment spread, and the same is still true of others. By a supreme irony, social patterns have turned one of the church's assets into a barrier. The church is a fellowship, and social aspects are important to its life. This is as it should be. But in our society we are "classified"—lower, middle, upper class, and in-betweens. At the office custodial, clerical, and professional staff function as a unit, but at the end of the workday they disperse to their separate worlds. The statistics on our chart demonstrate that Presbyterians claimed fewer of the clerical level, and even fewer of the custodial workers found their way to Presbyterian churches than did the "higher" strata of workers.

The "classes" do not normally socialize together, so that social aspect of the church's life often proves awkward. Education levels, economic standing, recreational activities, travel experiences—a plethora of differences conspire to make uneasy the social interaction in the congregation.

Few church members actively encourage friends and colleagues to worship with them, and crossing social lines to do so is even more rare. The janitor might make a much better asset to the church than the vice president, but then he is not "our kind of people."

A whimsical expression often heard in the African American church refers to the "big I's and the little U's." Captivity to society's standards is a real barrier to evangelism, as it makes fellowship in the church unnatural.

Racial Barriers

If the mythical visitors from Mars to the United States arrived on Sunday morning, they would witness processions of human beings streaming into certain buildings. There would be two distinguishable sets. One set would be of persons with little pigmentation in their skin. Then there would be others with the whole gamut of shadings. The inevitable assumption would be that these people are involved in different activities. There would be no reason to assume that they were worshiping the same God, and certainly not a clue that that God was a God of human unity and the goal of their religion to bring people together in love.

The intrusion of racial barriers into the life of the body of Christ has its similarities to the class divisions, but the separation in society is more drastic. This social virus involves animosities, suspicions, prejudices, brutal discriminations, and centuries of infestation. With the church existing in two worlds, it is impossible to sanitize the church against what its members live in their secular lives. People who are infected by noxious racial attitudes and practices do not drop them in the prayer of confession. They are toxins that have been brewing in church and society for centuries. People have been consciously or unconsciously schooled in them.

As a result, the old saying is still quite true: the Sunday morning worship hour is the most segregated hour of the week. The result is separate denominations and separate congregations within denominations.

These barriers were dramatized during the civil rights efforts of the 1960s, when highly publicized efforts of blacks to worship in southern white churches were met with hostility. But on those same Sundays, masses of white churches all over the nation would have responded with attitudes from cool tolerance to outright hostility to the presence of African Americans at worship.

When a private club refused to house a commissioner to the UPCUSA General Assembly in Indianapolis in 1959, the chairman of the housing committee, pastor of a leading church, said angrily that he was going to resign from the club. A colleague asked him what would have happened if that same Sunday an African American had requested membership in the church he pastored. He was silenced. The virus is national.

There have been notable changes, and across the country one finds churches ranging from "specklegrated" to reasonably integrated. The movement, however, as in institutions of higher education, has been almost totally that of blacks moving into hitherto white congregations. The sparseness of movement the other way is not caused by reticence of African American churches to receive whites, although there is some of that. It is the domination of race over religion, of fear over faith, that makes it difficult for whites. It is also difficult for people who have always been in the majority to adjust to minority status.

A situation in the world of higher education demonstrates this. *U.S. News & World Report*, in classifying 113 colleges in the southeastern United States, rated Spelman College, a historically black college for women in Atlanta, Georgia, as the top school in the Southeast.[1] But it is not only "historically" black. Despite its stellar status, it draws virtually no women of the majority race.

The socializing factor that we noted in the class barrier is an even more powerful negative force with race. Hovering over the scene like some horrible monster is the specter of interracial marriage. Paul sounds a caveat against "intermarriage": "Do not be mismatched with unbelievers. For what partnership is there between righteousness and lawlessness? Or what fellowship is there between light and darkness? . . . Or what does a believer share with an unbeliever?" (2 Cor. 6:14–15). But churches and Christians largely would prefer seeing a marriage between a Christian and a pagan than an interracial marriage between two Christians. Hence the kind of social intermingling that is integral to the church fellowship is actually a barrier.

This fear of intimate social contact is demonstrated in pastoral searches. In the Presbyterian Church, African Americans are employed in and elected to the highest levels of leadership. But regardless of their demonstrated pastoral abilities, their names seldom surface, and almost never find favor, when a congregation is searching for a pastor. The nature of pastoral relationships at their best makes the pastor somewhat a member of the family, and that is just too intimate.

[1] *U.S. News & World Report*, September 28, 1992.

As with the class barriers, the worship barrier is also a real power-ful negative factor. The differences in worship are not just in superfi-cial worship patterns. The meanings of the faith and the nature of worship are rooted in the lives of the believers, and as noted in the Scot-tish Presbyterian history, they are deeply rooted over time.

To understand the religious/worship situation it is necessary to un-derstand something of the history and nature of Christianity and of worship in the black setting. The term "African American" has only re-cently succeeded "black" in the lexicon of terms for this particular eth-nic group. The term is particularly fitting in speaking of worship, for black religion and worship blend the two strains—the African religious heritage and the exposure to Christianity in America.

The African was and is deeply religious, providing a fertile soil for rooting Christianity, whether in the North American slave life setting or the result of the work of the missionary in Africa. In slavery, however, it rooted in a very different life setting from that of those who introduced the slave to Christianity—living on the same plantations. The slaves had very different needs from those who introduced them to the "facts" of the faith. The facts of the faith and the meaning of the faith were highly divergent within the narrow confines of the plantation. There were two very different worlds, evoking two different expressions of the one faith.

In a life with neither satisfactions in the present nor any realistic hope for the earthly future, faith in a God of justice said to the slaves that, despite what they were told and what their circumstances dic-tated, this was not the way God meant for the world to be. So their preachers found in the exodus and in the justice messages of the Old Testament prophets that truth which sustained them, although life did not make sense.

The risen Christ of the New Testament was not a shadowy figure in the distant past, but a daily companion, giving support for the perpet-ual burdens of life. Many aspects of faith that might have been little more than theological concepts to those who taught them the faith were for them supports for sanity and survival.

The need for the assurance of Jesus with them in their miserable and fearful lives was expressed in song: "I want Jesus to walk with me"; "Oh my good Lawd, show me de way"; and "Steal away to Jesus" were pleas for the never-failing presence of Jesus.

In worship they poured out their souls over their burdens: "I'm so glad trouble don' las' always"; "Nobody knows de trouble I see"; "I'm troubled, I'm troubled, I'm troubled in min'(d), If Jesus don' help me I sho'ly [surely] will die"—all such songs testify to their faith as a life-support system.

The lives of these worshipers, totally dominated by others for the benefit of others, were drab and monotonous. Everything in their daily lives reminded them that they were slaves, but in their worship they were free! So there was an exuberance in their worship, expressing relief from oppression and repression. The "shout" songs were songs of jubilation: "I know de Lawd's laid his hands on me"; "Jubalee! Jubalee! O my Lawd, Jubalee!" Worship was filled with experiences that a not too reverent songwriter of more recent years described: "They're talking to the Spirit just like they see and hear it." This is the experience of the immanence of God that today's charismatics are reaching out for.

The preaching that the slaves received from white preachers was largely, "Believe in God and serve God by working for your masters and not stealing." But the freedom themes that the slave preachers found in the Old Testament told them differently. They knew that the love of the Bible contradicted the evil of slavery. Like John on Patmos, they had to conceal their messages in imagery that the worshipers understood and the master did not.

Again, songs were their codes. When they called for Pharaoh to let the people go, the master and the slave system were Pharaoh. Songs about crossing the Jordan expressed hopes for escaping across the Ohio. "Same train carry my mother, same train be back tomorrow" might mean the heavenly train or the hope of traveling the underground railroad with Harriet Tubman. The slaves' worship was expressive of the deepest longings and needs of their lives.

For both those who entertained clandestine hopes for freedom and for those for whom such hopes were just too unrealistic, there was another hope for release. The masters' preachers told them that if they obeyed their masters, when they died they would go to "nigger heaven," assuring them that even in heaven their earthly subjugation would continue. But from their slave preachers they got the biblical dream of heaven where they would have their rightful place with God. Again, their songs reflected it.

Looking from their cotton fields, seeing the master and mistress in their carriage going for a social call, they envisioned a heavenly carriage, swooping down from heaven, catching them up from the wretchedness of their lives, and they sang, "Swing low, sweet chariot, coming for to carry me home." Rejecting that inferior heaven that the white preacher described, they sang, "De Angels in Heab'n gwineter [going to] write my name." The miserable rags and bare feet would be things of the past, as they sang, "I got a robe, you got a robe, all God's chillun [not just the white ones] got a robe." The red clay glistened as they sang, "Yes, yes, yes my Lawd, gonna walk up de golden streets."

Their lives and yearnings were so far removed from the master's that he could not even hear the cries for freedom in the songs he enjoyed hearing.

This is as truly the background of black worship and religion as the rebellious history of Scotland is for Presbyterians and the struggles of and with the monarchy are for Episcopalians.

Emancipation brought small changes in the poverty-striken and oppressed lives of the technically free ex-slaves and their descendants. In the post-emancipation century, when the freedom dream seemed to turn to a nightmare, Christianity still had its vital meaning and worship its contribution to survival and sanity. If, in the words of a later black poet, James Weldon Johnson, the slave lived in a world in which "hope, unborn, had died," the freed slaves and their descendants lived in a world in which hope seemed to have been stillborn. The bright dreams of freedom were turned into nightmares, as satanic forces were unleashed against them, and the posts earlier occupied by erstwhile friends were held by those who were either indifferent to them or outright hostile. Every aspect of their Christianity and worship was still valid.

Even today, following the glow of the second emancipation, the civil rights movement, the problems of updated discriminations create profound insecurities. Even those who have done well educationally and economically are reminded by such events as the 1991–92 Rodney King episode that in many circumstances "justice" is just a word. Fiendish brutality by law officers was followed by a jury's finding that they had done no wrong.

With a half-acceptance in the society, they find themselves feeling like bastards in the family. The feeling of oppression is almost universal, whether conscious or unconscious.

Both the content and the emphases of the faith and the nature of worship continue to serve the spiritual needs of many troubled African Americans. Worship, preaching, and teaching that do not meet these soul needs are inadequate.

This is not to say that the basic faith and content of worship are different from that of other people. The elements of Christian worship are universal. But the needs to be served determine the shadings of the experience.

In counseling with white churches in changing communities, I have often heard the fear voiced that if they were to begin to integrate, they would shortly be overrun with blacks. I have sadly advised them that as long as they worship as they do, they should have no fear of being swamped by blacks.

My teacher, the late Jewish philosopher and religious leader Will Herberg, often used a quotation—"Whatever the U.S. is, the Jew is more so." He was saying that Jewish life was an intensification of the qualities of the national life, whether good or bad. The basic needs described in the slave's life were not different from the needs of people in general—they were just terribly accentuated by their oppression. Any assumption that the kinds of spiritual needs described here do not afflict the lives of all classes of people is wrong. Any absence of profound, passionate, prophetic declaration of the gospel of the liberating, sustaining God and the ever-present friend in Jesus leaves people terribly vulnerable. The most affluent and well-appointed lives are overwhelmed with fears, insecurities, captivities. The absence of profound and passionate proclamation of the liberating, sustaining God in worship and preaching leaves people crying silently, "Is it nothing to you, all you who pass by?" (Lam. 1:12).

In a seminar entitled "What the Black Church Has to Offer to the Wider Church," I took the position that one thing the black church and the black experience have to offer is a gospel for those bruised by a wide variety of life experiences—people of whatever social or economic class. The song "I want Jesus to walk with me" names a variety of life circumstances in which the sustaining presence of God is pleaded for. To infer that such needs are absent from the lives of white church members would be misleading. But when I have asked Presbyterian theologians what theology the church has for failure, meaning for those whom the secular successes have passed by, I have received furrowed brows and puzzled shakes of the head.

The value of what the black church has to offer may be in reserve for the time when it is more drastically needed. A preview of that time may be in evidence as people for whom life was "secure" are suddenly knowing the icy chills of insecurity. The cynical and pernicious accusation of President Reagan about people driving Cadillacs to pick up welfare checks has become painfully real as people who never dreamed of a day of poverty drive in BMWs to pick up food stamps. Do their churches have a message for them on Sundays? The widely heard "theology" of "Be good and God will bless you" coming over the air has its echoes in thousands of less widely heard sermons. The assumptions of a "good old Santa Claus" God and an eternal "morning in America" are leaving many Christians terribly vulnerable. They find themselves without an "invisible means of support."

The spiritual experience developed in the centuries "when hope, unborn, had died" will have wider meaning, and people will be drawn together by the cross. Some different qualities of worship experience may be needed, and pastoral counseling will have some new sets of problems.

An affluent Presbyterian church at the time of this writing has a number of previously affluent members who have suddenly lost their businesses or high-level positions. An African American pastor, one of a staff of several ministers, is being swamped with counseling demands. There seems to be an assumption that he may have something to offer that his colleagues, however well-intentioned and concerned, do not have. It may be that his experience is presaging a breakdown of barriers as the experience of blacks and the African American church bring theology and worship content that are desperately needed.

While looking at the failure of the majority church to reach out and effectively minister to African Americans, it must be admitted that there has generally been no more outreach from the black side of the church than vice versa. Looking back on pastoral days, the writer is painfully conscious that in training members to be contacts for the church on their jobs, he did not stress that they ignore racial boundaries. Like the elephant tied to a stake, his mind was restrained by the status quo and oblivious to the universality of the Great Commission.

This is not any blanket condemnation of traditional Presbyterian worship. Worship patterns that have served so well over centuries have basic soundness. But:

> The old order changes, yielding place to the new,
> Lest one good custom should corrupt the world.
> (Alfred, Lord Tennyson,
> *Morte d'Arthur*)

This has validity for religious expressions also. Where the nature of the worship and the proclamation are vital and alive, churches are growing numerically and spiritually. Nor is this to suggest that we search for some homogeneous church life and worship experiences. Backgrounds, social and psychological profiles, even economic status and educational levels *do* make differences. We can, however, borrow the best from one another.

Where Now?

The shrinking membership is one of the prices the Presbyterian and other churches pay for their class nature. Arising out of its Scottish background, the Presbyterian church looked to its own families for regeneration. It often excused itself from active evangelism outside its families by claiming that it produced its constituency through its family life and worship and church school. How that indifference to outsiders fitted in with a deep commitment to evangelism across the world was never clear. But seldom was the church aggressive in its own community. Now, with middle- and upper-class family size shrinking, the children are not there to be the replacements for the dying. The people who are having more children are not in our churches. The average of 4.1 infant baptisms per church per year over a span of twenty-three years (see table 1 in chapter 1) clearly shows the fallacy of the theory of internal evangelism! So we pay the price for our classism and racism.

But the church cannot sit still with its self-generated or imported problems that create the barriers. It must take seriously the unity of humanity that scripture reveals. That unity is sustained by science, for a person in need of a blood transfusion might find a blood match anywhere in the world.

Christ died for the salvation of all humanity. The Great Commission (Matt. 28:16–20) and the charge in Acts 1:8 cancel out the pagan concepts of class and race. The church is God's ministering agency to humanity—across the fence, across the street, across the railroad tracks, across town, across the world. God brooks no barriers.

While the church has hardly faced these old challenges, new ones of unpredictable proportions are rushing in upon us. Waves of recent immigrants with their fertility are creating a different and diverse society. Now that they are our neighbors it will be so easy to forget that they are the people to whom we have sent countless missionaries and in whom we have invested millions of dollars for them to "hear the word." Now "foreign missions" is in town. We can no longer just give some money and commission some brave people to go to the far places of the world. Foreign mission has become evangelism.

With our emissaries going to them, and with our domestic life not visible to the world through our living room picture window, they had only the witness of the life and work of those missionaries to personally validate what the gospel means to us. Now, as our neighbors and fellow citizens, they observe what the gospel really means to us. Koreans, who arise on Sundays to pray before dawn and gather at other regular times to pray, find it hard to understand that the church whose missionaries taught them to pray seems to do so little of it.

A Liberian, educated in a mission school, had had punctuality drilled into him seemingly ad nauseam. Coming to this country to study, he was at a bus station for a trip. He was astonished to find that the bus was late! His teachers had unwittingly given unrealistic impressions of what punctuality meant in the United States. How we relate to these new neighbors will determine what chance we have of effectively presenting the gospel.

Some come as Christians, the result of how the Holy Spirit has used the missionary efforts of the church. But there are barriers of culture that will force us to distinguish between the essentials of our faith and our own cultural accretions. In matters such as full selfhood for women, on which we cannot compromise, transition arrangements may need to be made. Immersed in this society, such Christians could not hold on indefinitely to their indigenous cultural practices. But to demand that the first generations submit themselves to the straitjackets of life as we understand it may not be the most Christian thing to do.

Virtually none will come with no religion. That does not free us from confronting them with the gospel. All the people to whom we have sent missionaries have had their own religions, but we have been convinced of the primacy of Christ. If they needed Christ "over there," they need Christ over here.

To break those barriers we need to learn a procedure that our overseas personnel are learning—"dialogue." It means talking back and forth about Christianity and their traditional faith. It means treating their religion and culture with respect. We do not in this process compromise the gospel, but we learn where they are in order to know how to explain the meaning of the Christian faith. This prospect can be staggering when we are not sure how to communicate with family, friends, and colleagues about Jesus Christ.

Dialogue may well go farther. There may be religious truths that we can learn from them. If we believe that the Holy Spirit is at work among all people, it is reasonable to believe that out of their religion and their culture they have perceptions of truth that can enrich our own. Thus our listening can be learning, not merely looking for openings to put our points across.

By midpoint in the twenty-first century, the population balances will have shifted radically. Present trends project that a substantial percentage of our population will be people of non-Christian backgrounds. The white population will still be in the majority, but a greatly reduced one. There are today more Muslims in the country than there are Episcopalians. Presbyterians are soon to be bypassed. What does this mean for Christ and the nation? Will Christians be a minority in this nation, as we are in the world? We shall either carry the gospel faithfully to our new neighbors or become a shrinking ghetto as the world passes us by.

Denominations are stressing the value of diversity. As that diversity gives room for varieties in worship patterns and in our social structure, there will be congregations of predominantly one race or another. But true evangelism must not bow tamely to society's artificial barriers, and especially not to class or race prejudices existing in the minds and spirits of Christians. For these are spiritual illnesses, not just social problems.

Breaking barriers is an essential function of the gospel. When the church breaks these bonds of social servitude, however, when it ceases to float with the secular tide and declares its independence from social restraints, it will pay the price. The price, ironically, may be further loss of numbers—at least for a while. But if it is done "on [his] account" (Matt. 5:11), it will be love in action—that is, evangelism. And it will be crossing barriers.

The rest we leave to God.

5

EVANGELISM IS
FAITH IN ACTION

If ever there was an unlikely candidate for "evangelism," the woman engaged in conversation with Jesus at the well qualified.

There were two elements in Jesus' faith. One was faith in God. The sun is in an enduring power relation with the earth, whether it, or its light, is seen or unseen. In a myriad of ways the sun is influencing and affecting the nature of earthly life. In the same way, God's love is in enduring, active relations with human life. Jesus knew that God was reaching out to Ms. Samaritan.

Jesus told Nicodemus that the Spirit controlled the power for rebirth, and related that power to the love that powered his mission.

Humanity is concerned with power. Human production, long dependent on physical power, gave way to mechanical, then electric, then nuclear power. These are powers of action, of motivation. Love has power to motivate.

Nuclear power has healing properties and can reach cancerous cells for therapy. Like the x-ray, love reaches deep to diseased soul-cells with its therapeutic power.

Jesus knew who the Samaritan woman was in terms of reputation and character. But he knew something else. He knew that the divinity breathed into humanity has a stubborn hold on life. He had faith in the woman's powers to respond. He saw, not the bedraggled, probably self-loathing creature who had sneaked out to the well rather than face her neighbors, but the transformed woman who would run excitedly back to the village with news about a man at the well.

When I was a boy making the morning fires in the fireplace, sometimes, as I cleared away the ashes, I would find some glowing embers from the fire of the night before. I would lay some kindling wood on the coals and blow gently until it glowed bright red and then burst into flame. Jesus knew that underneath the ashes of that misspent life the divine embers lay, awaiting the blowing of the Spirit. He had perhaps a couple of hours to blow on those long-buried embers, to fan them into a consuming flame.

Jesus had faith in the power of the love of God to redeem this miserable woman.

He had faith in the residual power of the woman to respond.

Evangelism is faith working—faith in God and in the power of God in humanity.

We are called to act in the dual faith in which Jesus acted. As we face people—all kinds of people—we dare to do so because of faith in God and faith in what God instilled in them. And faith in God includes faith that God can use us for the mission.

In Jesus' resurrection we have the ultimate assurance that God brings the dead to life. If we have faith in the resurrection, we should be armed with faith in what God can do in everything. That should remove any weakness and dispel any doubt that God can work a human transformation.

Jesus further challenges our doubts and hesitations by his injunction to go into all the world with the assurance of his presence. The healer of the masses, the raiser of the dead, the personal evidence of the power of God for renewed life, is with those who are willing to be his emissaries. That power works through those who have faith. Without that faith in God, we are easily discouraged by what we see in people to whom we should be confidently witnessing, bluffed by their goodness or their badness, as we shall see.

Weak faith blocks us off from two kinds of people. One can be represented by Ms. Samaritan. They may be characterized by such terms as "dissolute" and "disreputable." Some may be in our own social class, and others are not only of low morals but are "lower class." Our weak faith in God does not enable us to believe that God can transform the lives of such people. Like the Pharisees of old, we want nothing to do with them, and think that Jesus should stay away from them also (Matt. 9:10–13; Luke 15:1–2).

Jesus made it clear that he reaches out to the very worst. But we steer away from those people who are "too lost to be found." And if God can do anything with them, let God use X church, on the next street; they are not *our* kind of people.

Contact with many of them would not be normal or easy. The cultural, economic, and other differences (not necessarily race, this time) would make them ill at ease with us and us ill at ease with them. Do we, then, as a church have no responsibility for extending the message of the gospel to them? If First United Church of Christ, Second Methodist, or Third Presbyterian cannot do it, does the wider church—the presbytery, district, diocese, or classis—have responsibility to develop means of outreach to them?

Since they are "not our kind of people," how do we reach out to them?

Witness to
the Down-and-Out

We are not able to do directly everything we are called on to do. While person-to-person evangelism is the heart of the gospel in action, and we should not too easily excuse ourselves from finding ways to work at it, the institutional church has vital roles in carrying out other aspects of the witness.

Traditionally, the Salvation Army and assorted "rescue missions" concentrate on scooping people out of the gutter. Their activity does not, however, relieve other churches from any responsibility for the Mary Magdalenes and prodigal sons in the gutter. There are several approaches we may consider.

1. A congregation should study its setting and design some way to reach out to those beyond the pale of respectability.

2. A denominational unit, presbytery, district, or classis, may organize ministry in its area.

3. Churches in an area may develop an ecumenical approach.

4. Churches may give their financial and personal support to existing agencies such as the Salvation Army or rescue missions on a stated and continuing basis as part of their own mission.

There is no one way it may be done, but there is something deficient in the mission of a church that ignores "those people."

A special class of people, whose circumstances demand special ministry, are those in prison. Jesus spoke most strongly about ministry to those in prison, equating it to ministry to himself, with the greatest reward or punishment for obedience or disobedience (Matt. 25:31–46).

Just as we are shut off from some down-and-outers by social organization, we are shut off from prisoners by their incarceration, which makes it even easier to ignore them—although it actually makes it easier to reach them. Other down-and-out people are disseminated and hard to pinpoint. We know where the prisoners are and there are set procedures for reaching them, so we have even less excuse for not trying.

Every congregation in the nation is in the shadow of some type of prison, whether it is the local "lockup" or some major state or federal facility. Who are the men, women, and children who are incarcerated?

In local jails there are persons who have been arrested with highly different levels of evidence.

Many are innocent. Others have been arrested for misdemeanors or minor felonies but remain in jail simply because they do not have access to bail. With unconscionable delays in the court systems, they may remain jailed interminably, often losing their jobs and wrecking their families. Distressingly, they are exposed to life-damaging education from hardened criminals.

Young people are apprehended for varieties of real or suspected antisocial behavior and locked up with an undifferentiated prison population, exposing naive youth to a criminal environment that is foreign, frightening, and terribly demoralizing.

Many, adult as well as youth, find themselves disoriented in their new world and desperately needing moral and spiritual support. The church is shut off from them by the assumption that if they are there, they are criminals where criminals ought to be, and the only problem is that we do not have enough police to put more of them there or enough prisons to hold them. And in spite of the fact that Christianity is itself a "rescue mission," the church of Jesus Christ largely ends any sphere of activity at those terrible walls, or even at the courthouse doors.

It must be remembered that Jesus did not specify that we visit those who are not guilty. There was no presumption of innocence in his mandate. The assurance given to the thief on the cross adjacent to his was not predicated on his not having been a thief.

Those who are tortured by the fact that they are innocent, and those whose error was not venal in character but a defection from a normally steady life, are especially apt to be grateful for the sign that not all of society has turned against them. Not only they, but any prisoners, are inclined to be responsive to the hand and word of love.

The hand and word of friendship must not be manipulative. To capitalize on misery, distress, and fear in order to maneuver someone into "accepting Christ" is unchristian and may trigger a reactive rejection, not only of the "decision," but of the church itself. Again, the key is to offer love and the truth and the opportunity to let Christ correct their lives in the most sensitive, nondirective manner. Jesus would claim their souls.

The word and the ministry of love may well unite at this point. The word of love may be accompanied by providing necessary bail and other assistance. Such acts can easily be the saving grace to keep or put a life back on track, by freeing persons from the corrupting, brutalizing environment of the prison and aiding them to reenter normal society on a constructive basis. This too is evangelism!

A most meaningful and needed ministry to prisoners can be ministry to their families. This may take any of a variety of forms:

> Providing support for a family whose breadwinner is in prison
>
> Arranging transportation to a distant prison
>
> Providing counseling and support for children
>
> Providing legal counsel the family could not afford
>
> Other assistance that a concerned, creative church might devise

The terms "reform school" and "penitentiary" grew out of the concepts that there would be efforts to affect positively the characters of inmates. Most correction officers and departments deny any responsibility for improving the quality of life of those they supervise. With the destructive effect of their environment and with no influences for the better, it is inevitable that most people emerge in a worse moral and ethical state than when they entered the system.

Working at redemption of the imprisoned is a task for local churches, middle-level governing bodies, and denominations. It is a work for men's and women's organizations, locally and nationally. It is a ministry that should have its own trained cadre of clergy and laity, supported by the church(es) to enable them to be trained and to give full time to this frontline work. Chaplains as servants of the church should be standard ministries of the churches. Prison ministry is a prime area for local ecumenism.

In spite of Jesus' clear command to serve prisoners, it is a largely neglected area of ministry. The most prominent ministry is that of the Yokefellows, a Quaker-sponsored ecumenical ministry. The United Methodists, Presbyterians, and certainly some others have some program at the national level. There are numerous scattered local services to prisoners, largely only preaching and seeking decisions for Christ without the supportive ministries that give such decisions chances to develop.

Somewhat in a class by themselves are the Black Muslims, who put to shame a Christianity based on the belief that Jesus came to redeem the irredeemable.

When young convicts are shut in with hardened criminals, brutalized by fellow prisoners and often by prison staff, denied the ameliorating and humanizing influence that Christians and churches should be providing, it is inevitable that many become, themselves, hardened and brutal, that they reenter society with no skills, no friends, nothing to help them to readjust and avoid further infractions of the law; they tend, then, to become career criminals.

This is a loss of persons for whom Christ brought the offer of salvation and redemption. They are losses that the society cannot afford.

Their multiplication is a menace to the society. A society long geared to its own violence and ridden with often unjustified fears is willing to mortgage its freedoms and squander its resources in a super-police state and building, maintaining, and populating prisons. Failure to heed Christ's injunction is paid for in many ways that the society cannot afford.

Witness to
the Up-and-Out

We mentioned two classes that we are inclined to be shut away from. Ironically, in one sense they are contrasting populations. We have discussed the absence of ministry to the down-and-outers because our faith was not strong enough to believe that God could do anything with that crowd. And they are not our kind of people. The other group is the up-and-outers. Whereas we are not sure that Christ can do anything with that other crowd, we are not sure that these highly respectable people really need Christ. For they *are* our kind of people. They are so much our kind of people that they just seem to be nonchurch Christians.

There are two basic fallacies operative here. One is that we are misled by our focus on morals and ethics. We confuse Christianity with proper ethical living, and as we look at our families, friends, neighbors, and colleagues we see them living lives about like our own. To paraphrase what the wealthy young ruler said of himself, "All these things they have observed from their youth." We are not sure that these nice people *really need* Christ. Some of them are the pillars of the community—presidents of the Junior League, the Grange, the labor union, Rotary, the PTA, the Chamber of Commerce, even the mayor! We do not see substantial differences between their lives and our own, except that we claim to be Christian and relate to a church and they do not. This is a fatal fallacy.

We fear that we will offend them by implying that there is something lacking in their lives. But Christ did not die on the cross to accomplish what people could attain by being nice, respectable people.

Through the centuries, Christian ethical and moral teachings have so permeated the society that millions of people have accepted them as standards for living without having the profound faith and knowledge that are the rootage of the integrity of social order. They are living a rootless ethic, portraying a cut-flower beauty.

A second fallacy is assuming that, as we look at their external lives, what we see is the reality. Visiting a movie set where Western movies were filmed, my family and I walked down the middle of the street of the town—past the hotel, the general store, the saloon, the barber shop—all the way to the blacksmith shop at the end of the street. Then we crossed the sidewalk, going past what we had been looking at. Behind it all was nothing! Nothing except some stout props to hold it up. I knew then, experientially, what a "facade" was.

Assuming that behind all the poise, graciousness, and apparent integrity of our associates there is peace to match their poise is to contradict what we know about human nature. It is to contradict what scripture tells us about humanity. We know how respectability often conceals emptiness, meanness, brutality, fear, sensuousness, greed, loneliness—a multitude of sins and deficiencies. But we are immobilized by our assumption that behind the front everything is just what it appears to be. We are warned by God's injunction to Samuel, quoted earlier: "The Lord does not see as mortals see; they look on the outward appearance, but the Lord looks on the heart" (1 Sam. 16:7). The props that support the front may be a myriad of deceptions, just as the person who is "the life of the party" may be the loneliest person there. In dealing with human souls we must not be fooled by facades.

Experience should free us from this mental captivity. So many times we have seen those fronts fall away, revealing a shocking disparity between what we assumed was behind the front and the exposed reality. When with sickness, death, financial reverses, marital problems, disappointment with children, exposed alcoholism—when any one blow or combination of blows causes the bottom to fall out, the world to come crashing in, they are caught without spiritual resources, with no invisible means of support.

Then we say, "If we had only known!" We are not called to know, but to witness, the witness based not on what we know of people's lives but on faith in God to bring essential blessing to every life. We are to believe that even if that life had been all that we assumed it to be, without Christ it was a defective life. Our faith in God says that God has something for everybody. Otherwise, we are being fooled by facades. And eventually the props will fall.

A third fallacy grows out of the second. It is the assumption that many of those poised people are not aware of their needs and would not be open to guidance to find help. Many times, the conditions are there—waiting.

When Jesus went to Zacchaeus's house, we can safely assume that he was working with a man who had a bad conscience. Like this Sychar well conversation, we don't know how long the visit was. We may imagine that they talked all afternoon and Zacchaeus insisted that he stay for dinner, and that after dinner they continued into the night. Finally Zacchaeus showed Jesus to a guest bedroom. Zacchaeus, himself, found sleep impossible and after tossing and turning arose and went up on the roof.

Looking down on the darkened town, in his mind's eye he saw the people down there—the people whom he had cheated—and thought of the suffering he had caused. The effect, the infiltration of his mind and spirit, of the conversation with Jesus took hold, and finally he said to himself, "I'll do it!" Returning to bed with a liberated spirit, he fell into a sound sleep. At breakfast the next morning, he excitedly told Jesus of his life change and his resolve to make restitution where possible. (This imaginary version of Jesus' ministry to Zacchaeus is based on Luke 19:1–10.)

Jesus was working with a vulnerable spirit, and the Holy Spirit is still at work in lives in ways that we cannot know, preparing for what the Spirit has entrusted to us.

There are millions of Zacchaeuses, troubled by the failings in their lives. In Zacchaeus's case, he was publicly pegged by his occupation. Jesus knew Zacchaeus's corrupt life, and Zacchaeus knew that he knew it. Sometimes we know of the moral failures of our friends and must address them honestly. But most of our witnessing is simply based on the faith that, whatever the quality of life, God has something for it and what God has is needed. Thus we do our part and pray for the Holy Spirit to work in the Spirit's way.

There is really a third category of people that we evade. They are the "down and out up-and-outers." They are half concealed among us, wearing camouflage of respectability, but they are really just upper-class down-and-outers. A major group is the alcoholics—more numerous even in our congregations than our churches care to admit. We pretend they are not there, that we don't know that they arrive just as the service begins to avoid having to talk with anyone who might detect on their breath that last desperate drink before leaving the car. Or they habitually miss the Communion Sunday because the church insists on offering them the little sip of wine that would trigger a binge. Alcoholics Anonymous (AA) has taken basic Christian truth and shaped it to help those who want to be helped. They have taken the concept of Christian community to form the supportive fellowship that the alcoholic needs. AA does not seek to be a church for the salvation of souls. It addresses its part of the job, while the church often lets the destruction of life hide behind the camouflage of respectability. Like Jesus with Zacchaeus, we know the problem. Unlike Jesus, we look the other way. Many churches do provide meeting space gratis for AA chapters and thus participate in their mission.

The types of life deficiencies of respectable people are too many and varied to begin to identify. But they are the loads carried by millions of people who need to hear and respond to "Come to me, all you that are . . . carrying heavy burdens, and I will give you rest" (Matt. 11:28). Let us not cheat them because we are not privy to their burdens . . . or because we are too timid.

With the down-and-out and the up-and-out we must share the faith that Jesus exemplified with Ms. Samaritan.

We mentioned two kinds of faith at the beginning of this chapter. We should note here that a third element of faith is in the body of Christ— the church. This faith does not demand to be fed on instantaneous results. It is faith that God, who took time unimaginable to create a lump of coal, centuries to grow a sequoia tree, a season to grow a vegetable, can work patiently with the transformation of a human soul.

It is not necessarily a faith of "theological profundity," nor does it express itself in abstract theological language. It is an informed faith, a faith with a firm grasp of what scripture says and means.

The weaknesses of evangelism have been developing over a long period of time. During that same time, few congregations or families have had serious Bible study or extended prayer lives. Much Christian education, while dealing with important life issues, has made study of scripture itself peripheral. Much preaching has been rooted more in the social sciences, contemporary literature, and ethics than in scripture. The absence of extended Bible study handicaps the reception of that preaching which is biblical, because people have not "done their homework." Paul laments, "I fed you with milk, not solid food, for you were not ready for solid food" (1 Cor. 3:2).

The writer to the Hebrews goes farther: "For though by this time you ought to be teachers, you need someone to teach you again the basic elements of the oracles of God. You need milk, not solid food; for everyone who lives on milk, being still an infant, is unskilled in the word of righteousness. But solid food is for the mature, for those whose faculties have been trained by practice to distinguish good from evil" (Heb. 5:12–14).

Our faith is more than an intellectual faith; it is a faith of experience. I learned decades ago, in a high school physics class, that the nature of my body and the nature of water are such that if I relax, the water will support me. I even see it happen—to others. But my faith does not support my intellectual knowledge, so I can never relax. Therefore I can recount the facts of physics but cannot attest from experience. I cannot swim.

Those who have faith in what God can do for the down-and-out and the up-and-out are those who have intellectual knowledge that has been substantiated by experience. They may then be like Peter and John before the Council: "Now when they saw the boldness of Peter and John and realized that they were uneducated and ordinary men, they were amazed and recognized them as companions of Jesus" (Acts 4:13).

Evangelism is faith in action . . . action by those who by their words, works, and character give indication that they are companions of Jesus.

6

EVANGELISM IS
PATIENT WORK

How long was the conversation at the well? How long had it taken the disciples to complete their errand of buying food? Was it the normal haggling or was it more intense because of dealing with "those Samaritans"? There are, of course, no answers to these questions, but it is certain that the four-hundred-odd words of John's account give us but the barest gist of a lively, lengthy, and engrossing conversation.

To understand the conversation it is necessary to see it in its real context. It was not, existentially speaking, a conversation between a woman and the Messiah. It was a conversation between a personable young man and a woman of dubious morals in an isolated setting. Jesus knew, by her presence at the well in the heat of the day, who she was, and by that same social knowledge she knew that he knew who she was.

A group like Jesus and his disciples would carry their own skin bucket when traveling, but we must guess that after they had refreshed themselves on arrival the bearer of the waterskin had thoughtlessly carried it away with him. One might wonder whether Jesus purposely allowed the waterskin to go, because without it he had a conversation starter with whoever came to the well. And if someone did come, he knew what kind of person it would be. Only women carried water and only outcasts carried their water at noon. He did say, you know, "Be wise as serpents" (Matt. 10:16).

Jesus let down the barriers of custom and propriety by asking the woman for a drink. We can imagine that she drew the water and handed it to him in silence. After he had finished, she asked him why he had asked her for water.

According to strict social regulations, there would be no conversation between a man and a woman who were strangers to each other. Since he so casually departed from proper custom, she decided to explore that opening to see *really* why he initiated conversation. Remember, he was not the Messiah to her—not yet.

Jesus responded with the perfectly absurd statement that if the situation were reversed—if she had asked him for water—he would have given her living water.

Her response, a peasant woman talking not to the Savior of the world but to a young traveling Jew, could not have been serious. "Where do you get that water?" was not curiosity, but laughing sarcasm. She reminded him that, as great as their common father, Jacob, was, he had to depend on the well. She might well have asked if he had all that ability, why had he asked her for water? "Who are you that you can produce water independently of the well?"

Jesus then got more absurd as he replied that this water did the job only temporarily, but the water he could give would be a gushing internal spring, slaking thirst continually.

Now she really cracked up! She must have laughed until tears rolled down her cheeks. Could she possibly have said seriously, "Give me that water that I may never be thirsty or have to keep coming here to draw water?" Not a chance! More like, "O.K., Bud! Start the magic implant. I'd be glad not to have to drag out here in this hot sun every day. I can just see those old hags in the village snooping at night, trying to see where I get my water."

This "alternate reading" is contrary to the traditional interpretation, as we read from our perspective of knowing who Jesus really was. But to this woman he was not the miracle worker from Galilee who made wine out of water, so to read the conversation taking seriously what she says is to rob the event of some of its rich meaning.

She was having fun with this young man who was saying these absurd things, and responded the only way any normal person would, more with amusement than amazement. Jesus, however, is patiently moving toward some point of deeper contact.

When her laughter had subsided and she was wiping away the tears, Jesus suddenly shifted the direction of the conversation, suggesting that she go and bring her husband. She responded (was it curtly or coyly?) that she did not have a husband. He then made a quick thrust, telling her that she had had a series of husbands and was now living with a man who was not her husband.

With this disorienting statement, she was thrown off balance. She knew that this man had never been in her village—how did he know this much about her? Her flippancy deserted her. He was getting too close for comfort. She said, "I see that you are a prophet," and probably was serious, since she could think of no other way that he could know her life's story. She regained her composure, however, and tried a diversionary tactic to get the focus off her life. She sought to use a tactic that is still in use—if somebody is talking too seriously about Christianity, start a religious argument.

A pastor visited a man, and they had friendly talk about various things. But the minute he steered the conversation toward spiritual concerns, the man would invariably ask, "Why does the Lord's Prayer say, 'Lead us not into temptation'? Would God lead anybody into temptation?" It was not a question for which he sought an answer. This is a trap to be avoided. Religious arguments seldom promote evangelism.

With the Mount Zion–Mount Gerizim controversy raging between Jews and Samaritans, Ms. Samaritan was sure that she could get a diversionary argument. Jesus avoided the argument and moved the conversation to a higher level, responding as though he might be talking to the religious leaders at the Temple in Jerusalem. Acknowledging the controversy, he proceeded to discuss worship at the highest level. "God is spirit, and those who worship him must worship in spirit and truth" (John 4:24).

He gave her an answer, but he did something else. In talking to her earnestly about matters of spiritual truth, he electrified her. He showed respect for her as a person. How long had it been since anybody had spoken to her as though she had any value? When was the last time a man treated her as though she was not just a "thing"?

Her spirits soared. In memory she reached far back beyond the ugliness of her life to something that had meaning in days when things were different. She murmured something half-forgotten: "I know that Messiah is coming. . . ." This woman . . . this woman who had been dragged through the muck and mire, robbed of dignity and a sense of worth, . . . this woman who at the beginning of the conversation may have had hopes of selling her body, is transformed! What a transformation! How long did it take? How long and how patiently did Jesus work to stir those embers lying hidden under the ashes of a misspent life?

The woman who had slunk out of the village at noon to avoid her neighbors is now ready to fly back into town and stun them with her transformation. It had not been accomplished with four-hundred-plus words. It had been patient work!

Evangelism is patient work.

Earlier we noted that we live in an "instant" society. But in dealing with the eternities of the human soul, patience is a God-given, essential virtue. Patience in the individual expresses human characteristics. Patience in the institution expresses itself in such principles as organization.

Organization—National

Organization in the church is structural, and involves the total church. One of the several false dichotomies in the life of the church is "top down" versus "grass roots." In this as everywhere, the ministry is integrated from top to bottom. A truism is that evangelism is done at the local level. Repeatedly we have spoken of lessons that can be learned from the commercial world. The great chain stores have headquarters, regional headquarters, warehouses, transportation systems, and multiple other functions, but sales are made in the stores. The stores could not function, however, without the operational system. The key word is "integrated." This is not to say that no single church could function apart from a denomination. But no lone congregation could carry out the breadth of the work that Jesus assigned. There should be creative help from the denomination, but the creative and imaginative work of the local congregation is the key to evangelism.

There is a vital role for the "organizational above" as well as the divine above. The national church has the responsibility to assemble a staff of the most competent, dedicated, and experienced persons to give guidance. They do this through:

Developing strategies
Developing materials

Providing field leadership

Organizing training events

Working with middle-level administrative units

Responding to expressed needs from the field

Performing the bee/butterfly function of cross-pollination, sharing across the country things that are working

Learning from its erstwhile mission churches around the world

Doing research in the field of evangelism

Having continuing conversations with other U.S. denominations for mutual enrichment

Study of world evangelization through the World Council of Churches Department of Evangelism

Organization—Local

All the work of the national organization is done to be at the service of the local church as it carries out its humanly impossible mission—to take the gospel to the whole world, beginning at home.

Realizing the serious nature of the decision people will be challenged to make, the church's approach should be long-range and patient. It involves persons, plans, group dynamics, equipment, and material, as well as the dynamic of patient prayer.

Whatever the church's functioning structure, evangelism should be deeply rooted in it. The governing boards should have ultimate responsibility, but in many cases it is necessary for leadership to be delegated to some subgroup that will concentrate on supplying it. It may be large, with subcommittees in large churches, or may be two people in the small congregation.

Procedures

In "Going out of the Way" (chapter 3) we noted that for patient, long-term work, the Spirit uses files, computers, plans, and organization.

At that time we left those names, acquired by various means, on file cards and in computers. What next?

We must remember what it is we are about. We speak about simply "joining the church" or, at a deeper level, about "conversion." Many of the persons we have reached are struggling with a total reorientation of life. This experience is establishing a new center of life—Christ will be replacing self. When the center changes, all priorities are shuffled. It changes lifestyles, economics, time schedules, pleasures, and relationships. It often means accepting a new worldview.

Such life changes will often develop slowly. A plane seatmate regaled me with accounts of his soul-winning successes. They had happened on short hops like ours, in customers' offices after a business transaction was done, with all sorts of casual acquaintances. I admire him for his dedication and cannot question the validity of the conversions. But we must remember Jesus' warning about quickly sprouting, rootless plants (Matt. 13:3–9, 18–23).

Jesus said to Nicodemus that he must have a new birth. There are differences between the physical and the spiritual births. Physical birth is never accomplished without a gestation period. The fetus plays no conscious participatory role in the process, and the time of the process is reasonably predictable. The spiritual gestation process may be sudden or of indeterminate length. But a fundamental difference is that the one being spiritually born plays an active and determinate role in the process, willing it to happen or not.

The evangelism committee understands the nature of what the church should be doing. Its assignment is not to "do the evangelism," but to lead the congregation into doing its work of evangelism. Evangelism is not a "program" of the session—it is a function of the entire church.

The evangelism leadership, including the pastor, should arrange strategies to identify people in the community who are not spiritually involved, by:

      Checking families of church members

      Seeking information from members

      Systematically gathering information from visitors

Discovering families of children involved in various church
activities

Doing community censuses

Advertising in the various media

Hospital and jail visitation

Following up on pastor's contacts in personal and community service

Interesting persons in church organizations, programs,
and community services—organizations which became
vestibules for entry

Cultivation

When families milked cows and churned milk to make butter, there
were times when in the churning process little flecks of butter would
appear in the milk but would not cohere. Traditional lore was to pour
a little warm water in the milk, and shortly lumps of butter would
form. Key work of evangelism is to develop processes for the warming,
moving persons toward firm decision making. These may include:

Enrolling them in Bible study and study of spiritual truth

Arranging home visits by well-chosen communicators,
clergy and lay, to help them face the question, "What
shall I do about Christ?"

Finding various ways to sensitively expose them to the
warm and loving fellowship of God's people. We move
from data to doing

Interacting with the vertical structure of the denomination, the local
church has to be the active agency, fired by the Holy Spirit and by love for
God and humanity, in order to reach out to people with love and concern.

A puzzling contradiction is that there are many churches and church
members who are excited about "foreign missions," but seem to have
no sense of compulsion to do that mission in their own communities,
to their own families and neighbors. This does not escape Christians in
what we call "missionary lands." Earlier reference was made to the fact

that around the world Christians are asking why some of our people are so eager to send missionaries across the world to help them when they are not carrying the gospel across the street, especially when the church is growing faster in many other places than at home. Our indifference to Jerusalem makes mockery of us in Samaria and to the ends of the earth (Acts 1:6–8).

In our look at "Compulsion of Love" (chapter 2) we were reminded that God's love is for the whole of humanity, and that places all people in our focus. In "Crossing Barriers" (chapter 4) it was pressed upon us that we have no license to pick and choose to whom we carry the message of God's love. Now we ask ourselves: How do we carry out our mandate where we live?

The answer is complicated by the fact that those to whom we would carry the message of God's love are so varied in terms of religious concepts and experiences and in relationship or nonrelationship with the church. They may include:

> People with no knowledge of the gospel and only vague notions about the church
>
> People who have grown up within the family of the church, but have presently no relationship, and possibly no understanding of it
>
> Those who have been members of a church, whether supporting or nominal, but who have broken with or drifted away from it
>
> Those who claim to be Christians but who have no relationship with the church

Beyond these relational categories are the varieties of life quality. They are respectable, criminal, illiterate, educated; in "high society," in the "gutter"; depraved, in that they cheat their employees, bosses, or customers; depraved, in that they are adulterers, prostitutes, or consort with prostitutes, male or female. They are those who would not lift a hand to harm another person, but will stab a person with their tongues. They are content as they are, and desperately unhappy with themselves. They are angry with themselves, or angry with the world—or both.

In short, our assignment is to the people whose lives are separated from God, and who are thus living in hells or in hells in the making. They are people desperately in need of the love of God, but they may not know it—or even know that such love exists. But for the assurance of the work's being God's work and the Holy Spirit the director of operations, we would be immobilized by knowing what our assignment really is.

Merely scanning the scope and complexity of our assignment sends a message that it demands dedication and patience. My seatmate evangelist had a packaged presentation that he gave, and he asked the other person to accept Jesus as Savior on the spot. Those of us who shy away from that type of presentation cannot write off the power of the Holy Spirit to use that approach. Persons so approached may have a memory of childhood that makes them receptive, or may at the time of the conversation be in the midst of some experiences that make them open to the offer of God's love. With the multiplicity of human predicaments, however, and the intricate webs of woe, the Holy Spirit is more likely to design long-range plans for saving people from themselves and from society.

In part, evangelism is a "To whom it may concern" general message. But it is also a focused message, "tailor-made" for individuals and groups. We start at the true beginning—with children.

Evangelism with Children

Noting one day a very familiar sign—EARLY LEARNING CENTER—it struck me that the caption might well be before every home that has children. The beginnings of evangelism are the responsibility of parents. In the Presbyterian Church (U.S.A.), in infant baptism parents commit themselves to "live the Christian faith and to teach that faith to your child." Other denominations have ceremonies of blessing or some other spiritual rite. But where there is no formal ritual, parents who are Christian are under obligation to rear their children as Christians. It is all too common for parents to say later that they do not wish to "force religion on their children," but want them to make up their own minds about religion, thus depriving them of the teaching of home and church and revoking the vows they made to God. Make up their minds they certainly will! But if they are left to make their decisions deprived of Christian teaching, they are crippled in decision making, and the parents have abdicated their formative leadership to the secular forces of society.

In the infant baptismal ceremony, the congregation vows to assist the parents and to provide the children with the teaching and atmosphere that will be conducive to their spiritual growth. Like some parents, a disturbing number of churches renege on their vows to God. Like some parents, Christian education departments often have an almost paranoid fear of "manipulating" children, inducing a paralysis toward influencing children toward faith.

There are manipulative ways of dealing with children, and avoiding them is wise. But not to proclaim the faith at all for fear of doing it in a poor way is to rob children of their birthright and forsake the church's vows.

The long gestation period for a child to make the crucial decision begins in a home in which family worship provides early and subconscious images for children of a special book, some language, activities, and relationships whose meanings will evolve with time.

The exposure continues in the relation to the church, in the various experiences there, as the church school augments what happens at home. That sets up interplay between the home, the congregation, and curriculum writers and leadership educators.

In addition to Bible study and other subjects, the Christian education curriculum should include study activities for parents as parents. Ability to conceive and give birth does not qualify us for parenthood. Parents have a dual role in relationship to the church education program. One is to avail themselves of every opportunity for their own spiritual growth and their growth as parents. The other is to expose their children to the church's teaching. The church school should be a family affair, as parents' involvement silently teaches the children that it is important. If parents drop the children off and do not participate, they say to their children, "This is just something for children," and children will look forward to being dropouts like Mom and Dad. If Mother takes the children and Father wanders along for church, the boys see that it is something for women and children. They are being patiently taught—the wrong way.

Christian education is exposing children to an expanding grasp of truth as the ability to understand it grows. An important part of that growth should take place as the family worships together. A disturbingly large number of churches deprive the children and the rest of the family of what should be a family experience by removing the children for other teaching activities. It is a deprivation, though at what level beyond the nursery they should be out of the service is a sticky decision.

At what age should children be encouraged to make a decision? Denominations vary so widely at this point that no position is taken here. Some welcome decisions as early as six years of age. Others, especially those who baptize them as infants, lean toward eleven or older and provide church membership training for them. A problem with such training is that some who are not ready may feel under pressure to take action for which they are not ready.

The responsibility of the church is not just for children whose family relationship puts them in touch with the church; it is to reach out to all children. This involves "going out of the way," and the church bus can be an evangelistic tool.

Reaching children for Christ is patient work!

Evangelism with Youth

The term "loss of members" seems to carry the connotation of people actually leaving the church. We have seen that the disappearance of members may not play the part in statistical reduction that it might seem to. There is, however, one group of which there has been a virtual hemorrhage. That is the youth.

Some decades ago, some denominations that had had excellent youth programs became imbued with the idea that the youth should not be categorized as such, but should be full members of the church. Youth curricula and organizations were discarded. They forgot all that secular and Christian education and psychology had taught about stages of development.

At the age when the world of the youth was widening, when they had new and more perplexing questions, when life-shaping decisions had to be made, when they were going through the torturous struggles for identity, and with all the intensity of peer pressure on them, they were deprived of the materials designed for their needs, deprived of the leaders and meetings for dealing with their needs—their level of needs.

During the same period some of the college and university denominational fellowships changed their nature and became ecumenical. They were valuable in themselves, but the very nature of being ecumenical reduced the sharpness of their focus. Youth still in need of help with faith formation found that aspect dropped in favor of broad social concerns. Such emphases were needed, but not to the extent of ignoring that many college students were still struggling for a meaningful personal faith.

At the same time they were thrown into new challenges to their often immature faith. Many encountered university-level professors with worldviews that had no place for God or prayer, and faced some respected academics, often even in church-related colleges, who introduced ideas ranging from skepticism to scorn about their faith. Many were not equipped for the challenge. They came away empty.

These developments were only some of the factors that resulted in the loss of generations of youth. Increase in part-time employment made them less available. Fast-food jobs conflicted not only with youth activities but often with basic worship itself. Mistaken family priorities made band and twirling camps more important than church summer conferences. Even affluence often became a negative factor.

Breakdown in the family itself should not be overlooked as a major factor. Young people were disillusioned by the disparity they saw between the teachings of the church and home and the lives of parents and other church members.

This dismal history is recounted merely to set the stage for what must now be done.

What about today's children and youth? They continue to move through those crucial years of church and family life, and "now is the day of [their] salvation" (2 Cor. 6:2). An Old Testament story tells of a man who was set to guard a prisoner. The prisoner escaped and the man reported to the king, "While your servant was busy here and there, he was gone" (1 Kings 20:40). The church must not lose sight of its families' children and youth while it searches for the strayed.

Evangelism and Christian education should be working in close relationship, all the way from curriculum writers to the local church. "Christian education" that does not have as a primary focus stirring the minds and hearts of people for opening their lives to Christ is misnamed. This is not to discredit the broad range of growth areas with which Christian education must deal. But if evangelism is the church's priority, it has to be the priority of the church's Christian education program. "What do you know about Christ?" and "What do you believe about Christ?" are steps to "What will you do about Christ?"

Essential to ministry with children and youth is in-depth study of their development and their world. Many encounter in their daily lives social and moral conditions most of their elders cannot imagine. On the streets, at school, on the playground, they are subjected to language, ideas, and experiences of which their parents cannot conceive. The current rap music is a prime example. To most adults it is just an offensive sound; to young people it is bringing messages. While it is reported that some of it brings sound messages about the society, most of it seems to be degrading filth, drummed into the minds of impressionable children and youth. This is merely symbolic for many aspects of youth life that must be understood as the church plans ministry to them.

If we have faith in the activity of the Holy Spirit, the most distressing and dismaying factors relating to young people may at the same time be sources for hope and confidence. The bizarre and vagarious directions in which they are frantically seeking meaning testify to their deep awareness of need and their longing for meaning. The craving for junk food is a misdirection of the craving for nourishment.

At a church mission boarding school we had numerous students from the streets of cities. Along with other wholesome elements, we sought to give them a balanced diet, only to face protests. At home their parents just gave them money for much of their food, and they had developed the taste for foods that were more damaging than nutritious. Our challenge was not only to provide them with good food, but also to try to create in them a taste for it. How to do this with our youth is one of the monumental tasks the church faces. It demands endless patience.

Jesus saw beyond the Samaritan woman's personal life to the basic good in her that could be reached. The church must have faith in the potential of young people to respond to the best.

To inspire youth to respond to its message, the church will have to match its quality of life to its teaching. "What you are speaks so loud that I cannot hear what you say" may be trite, but it is often true. On a street in a small Western town, a young woman asked me for some kind of financial help. She seemed intelligent and educated, so I asked her how she happened to be in that situation. Over cups of coffee, a long story spilled out. She had been brought up in a Christian (that is, "church related") home. As she became aware of the discrepancies between what her church and parents taught and what she saw in church and parents, she had become so disillusioned that she had cut her ties and was seeking for a new direction, though she knew not just what that would be. The church will have to contend with its own history to reach many young people.

The basic message to youth is the basic message of the gospel—love. God loves you. The church loves you. I love you. You are called on to love. Many have the feeling of being unloved and may not even know how to accept love. We are learning, to our dismay, how many of the "best homes" are simply houses, sheltering distressing varieties of human irregularities.

Many young people have all the love that "money can buy." In spite of financial security, they suffer from terrifying insecurities. Lacking strong convictions, they are vulnerable to varieties of pressures. The satisfaction of their hungers is the Bread of Life. The cure of their murderous maladies is in the hand of the Great Physician. Our children are not to be tinkered with by handing them spiritual junk food or spiritual patent medicines.

Some groups have shown success with youth, whether they are just wandering or have "gone off the deep end." Certain para-church organizations reach young people, their lifesaving efforts at the same time directing tremendous spiritual energies into creative spiritual activities.

The Black Muslims are changing the lives of prisoners and of drug users on the streets. Jesus spoke sorrowfully of "you of little faith." Much of the church qualifies for that description.

We must start where these youth are, which will often be a jarring, jolting experience. Their hostilities, their anger, their language, their lifestyles can put us through some excruciating experiences, so that the patience we need may be in danger of being destroyed at first contact.

Jesus started with water, the well, and a jeering woman, but he had a plan. Often we will face such strange and even frightening situations that we will have no plan, only faith and a prayer.

"The Submarine Church," a group of hostile, angry young people, moved in on the UPCUSA General Assembly in 1970 with the intention of disrupting its proceedings. Moderator William ("Bill") Laws led the Assembly to agreeing to giving them time on the agenda. They vented their anger, hostility, vulgarity, and profanity on the Assembly. Moderator Laws then asked them, since they had been heard, to give him a chance by hearing him, and invited them to worship where he was preaching on Sunday and to have lunch with him afterward. The long conversation there ended only when an unavoidable responsibility called him away. I know nothing of the long-range results of the encounter, but it was an example of the church's meeting a group of young people where they were, with all the discomfort it brought.

The "patience" for reaching youth is structural and organizational. That patience demands redeveloping trust among congregations, middle governing bodies, and national leadership, because only together can the church effectively address these life-and-death concerns.

To analyze and strategize for the ominous issues relating to youth and to develop program and materials to meet their need will demand a high involvement of funds and personnel. A task force is needed, involving people such as the following:

> Laypeople (including youth) and pastors from churches with successful programs and evangelism for youth
>
> Denominational staff of evangelism and Christian education from various levels
>
> General educators, psychologists, and sociologists/social workers with strong Christian convictions
>
> Consultants from some parachurch organizations
>
> Youth consultants who are outside the faith

Such a task force, with such an ongoing responsibility, demands substantial financing, in a day when denominations that need it most are in dire straits for national funds. But, considering the task and the woeful thought of what is happening now and will only escalate in the lives of young people, who can put a dollar figure on the effort? or on the cost of not doing it?

The issue is vital enough to the lives of young people, the church, and the nation so that it warrants seeking major foundation or other private financing. An ecumenical approach would improve the possibility of such support.

Reaching youth on behalf of Christ is patient work—personally and organizationally.

General Evangelism

Although we are putting great stress on the special evangelism of children and youth, this is not to imply that they are not included in plans for general evangelism. They are. Emphasis was put on evangelism for children and youth because of their special status. But they are part of the general evangelistic approach.

In "Going out of the Way" (chapter 3), emphasis was laid on getting people into the worship experience. Our human efforts there expose them to the workings of the Spirit in that setting. In worship they

Learn some of what the faith is about

Are exposed to the intellectual and emotional impact of worship

Experience the fellowship of the church

Begin to develop an activity pattern

Become introduced to scripture

These are intertwined inseparably, and in the service of the Spirit their values are intensified. They give the Spirit the opportunity to "blow where it chooses" (John 3:8).

In chapter 5, "Faith in Action," we saw that Jesus had faith in the power of God to touch Ms. Samaritan and in her ability to respond. To these elements of faith in God and in people we add another—faith in the worship and fellowship of the church to be the effective instrumentalities of the Holy Spirit.

Not every church has electrifying preaching or a choir with the ability to transport worshipers into sublime moods. The setting may be inelaborate and the pews half filled. But it is the church of our Lord Jesus Christ. The word read and preached is the gospel. The hymns, anthems, and solos are expressing the faith in the penetrating art of music. The people, with all their imperfections, are the people of God. Our assignment is to bring people into that worship in the faith that that God uses even pedestrian sermons, music deficient in art, and incomplete Christians to draw others to the faith.

Church members may feel that there is nothing in their worship service that is likely to encourage anybody to respond. They cannot evaluate the potential effect of their church's worship by its impact on themselves. The "old, old story" that may have become stale news to them may be fresh and exciting to their neighbors, if they are exposed to it.

With the continuing immersion of active members in the life of the church, there is danger that its very humanness may cause them to forget that it is not merely a human organization. It is the body of Christ, and that faith should overcome any hesitations we may have about its worth.

We have already deplored our short-span mentality. In our impatience with people's failing to respond as quickly as we would like, we become discouraged. Faith tells us that through their continued worship, Christ may lead them to commitment. Remembering the life-changing implications in that decision, we must give them time to grow toward it.

A hen keeps her eggs warm for about twenty-one days, or an incubator does the job for her. Those that are fertile produce little chicks. Worship should be an incubative experience in this same manner, conducive to persons' in due time saying yes to God. It is patient work, but care must be used. The hen cannot overheat the eggs, but the incubator can, and this spoils the eggs. A danger with hens, though, is that some will wander away from the nest and allow the eggs to chill. That certifies no life to come. We can overheat our prospects by insensitivity or chill them by indifference.

Like Isaiah, in some worship experience (Isa. 6:1–8), like Samuel during some sleepless night, like Paul going the wrong way on one of

God's one-way streets, they may get the call. Continuing gentle and sensitive invitations to worship are integral to patient cultivation.

The supermarket in its advertisements made it clear that they wanted us to buy. Churches are not so clear that they want people to make decisions for Christ and/or to become members of the congregation and the universal church. Homiletics of a half century ago included "hortatory" sermons—sermons that exhorted worshipers to action. Hearing sermons across the country, one seldom finds hortatory sermons or even hortatory elements in sermons. Paul's exhortation, "We entreat you on behalf of Christ, be reconciled to God," is seldom heard in worship, and hymnal revisions are gradually reducing the number of hymns that voice calls to discipleship.

Members in a number of denominations would think it strange, or even inappropriate, to have an invitation given from the pulpit for persons to leave their pews and come forward to signify their desire to accept Christ or to unite with the congregation. Many other denominations and most African American Christians would consider it wrong not to give that invitation. It is considered an integral part of the worship experience. The birth of a new Christian and the declaration for membership in the congregation are considered parts of the life of the church family. Mention was made earlier of a lady who responded one Sunday to the invitation to discipleship. There were probably thirty or more people present who had been involved in her nurture over about seven years, and scores of others who were aware of the outreach to her over the years. Her response was a dynamic spiritual experience for the congregation. One wonders whether any church should be deprived of this experience of worship, evangelism, and fellowship.

We owe the Holy Spirit all the human cooperation we can give: friendly ushers seating people amidst a friendly congregation; a choir that is its best because people who should be in it are, and whose members realize that their role is central to worship and so do their best and practice as required; liturgists who are prepared for their ministry and who read, rather than mumbling the scripture; and a preacher who, though not necessarily a great preacher, is the best preacher that homiletic skills and training make possible.

If there are a hundred people at worship on a Sunday, the hour they spent in preparation and arriving, the hour to which many congregations limit the Spirit, and a half hour getting back home, there will have been two hundred and fifty human hours invested. Those who lead in worship have the human responsibility to make that investment worthwhile. If it is made so, God can use it for reaching out in love—to the committed and to the uncommitted.

Following Up

Plans for maintaining contact and preventing the files and computers from being graveyards of evangelistic potential are the next step in the patient work of evangelism.

Integral to cultivation is maintaining contact. It may seem quite routine, but done sensitively it has real value. Under the careful guidance of the evangelism committee, and subcommittees if necessary, or the assigned leader in the very small church, the cultivation begins.

With first-time visitors at worship, it begins immediately. The ideal is for the records to be checked after worship and for some member to call by telephone or personally that same day to express pleasure at their having joined in the worship. If a personal call is not made that day, one should be made during the week if at all possible. A Canadian researcher I heard speak reported that the chances of success are greater:

The sooner a contact is made

If the initial contact is made by a layperson. The pastor, then, becomes the follow-up, rather than the primary caller.

But better the pastor first than for nobody to call or that it be delayed indefinitely.

Carefully orchestrated communication begins. The three ready means of communication are all used—the telephone, the mails, and personal visits, lay and clergy. A running record should be kept.

Efforts should be made to keep track of participation in worship until attendance becomes reasonably regular. In the small congregation this will be simple and uncomplicated, but at least some member of the board or designated member should be responsible for keeping some

records. In larger churches, a system is needed for ascertaining attendance. The most popular is the pew pad, circulated at what is often
misnamed the "fellowship time"—misnamed because it leads visitors
to expect more than generally occurs.

A more effective technique, if congregational resistance can be overcome, is the use of a general attendance registration card, placed in
both the bulletin and the pews, with stub pencils, if practical. Visitors
feel more at ease registering if they see that all worshipers are doing so.
Such registration of parishioners can be of great value if checked and
recorded regularly. It gives the church a jump on the "membership
slide" toward the back-door exit. This is with the supposition that organized follow-up is provided. Without some such record keeping and
follow-up, it is inevitable that some members will fade out, unnoticed
until it is too late. The Canadian researcher mentioned earlier holds
that the single greatest reason for defections from the church is indifference on the part of the church. The absence of continuing information may often be a reason.

Cultivation should be done through various fellowship experiences.
Every organization in the church has the potential of being a
"vestibule" to facilitate entry into the faith and the church. In one
church the women's religious book club attracted women with literary
interests, numbers of whom moved on into the membership.

In the same church, a monthly men's bean and dog supper attracted
men of the community to their meetings around civic issues. Getting to
feel at home in the basement, men began to find their way to the sanc-
tuary.

A dedicated choir may attract members who will literally sing their
way into the church. But they must not blend so well that their tenta-
tive status is forgotten and cultivation ceases.

Youth organizations at all levels are often entry points, not only for
the youth but for their families.

Athletic and sports activities are excellent vestibule activities.

None of this works automatically. The evangelistic leadership keeps
the membership alert to encourage people not to stop in the vestibule.

As important as we claim involvement in worship to be, it is but a
part of a wider long-range process. We now turn to that process.

We spoke earlier of the traditional way to make flecks of butter cohere, when churning butter, by pouring a small amount of warm water into the milk. Before long the flecks would gather to form a mass of butter.

Many people in the files and computer will be in varying stages of indecision. The church must learn and use every spiritually sound technique to encourage them to action.

There are many ways to seek to do this, and the committed congregation will find some. The national leadership should be helping by creating techniques and doing its work of cross-pollination across the country.

The Lay
Visitation Ministry

In the first chapter we described the lay visitation ministry of several decades ago. It had mixed results because it was done well and done poorly. It is a sound method and deserves use.

It is a continuing action/reflection/prayer type procedure. It is based on Jesus' principle of training his disciples and sending them out on a mission in pairs.

It begins with congregational leaders studying the method. Unfortunately, not much in the way of materials from the earlier experience is available.[1]

The work has already begun in churches that have documentation on people in the community who are not in the faith or are not active with a church. It moves now from data to action.

A few workers are selected—carefully, prayerfully. Volunteers are not solicited. Commitment and enthusiasm are needed, but these have to be matched with some other indispensable characteristics, personality traits, knowledge, and skills. Jesus called everybody to follow him and calls all to witness in some way. But he trained and commissioned a smaller cadre for certain work.

For this work people are needed who:

Live in a way that commends them as dedicated Christians

Have a good general knowledge of scripture

---

[1]One book is *The Practice of Evangelism*, by Bryan Green (New York: Charles Scribner's Sons, 1951). It is out of print, but can be found in some seminary libraries.

Have understanding of the faith

Communicate well

Listen well and are not inclined to be overtalkative

Are tactful and sensitive

Have a sense of humor

Have an enthusiasm about the faith and the church; and

Are "not easily provoked" (1 Cor. 13:5, KJV)

Stated thus, this list may seem to demand paragons of virtue scarcely to be found. But these traits are found in varying combinations in a reasonable number of Christians. The pairing process can match strengths and weaknesses.

In the beginning, it is better to risk getting too few than to make poor selections. As strong workers are developed, others can be added and paired with them.

Selection would be by the evangelism leaders in cooperation with the pastor. The pastor would then recruit them individually, introducing the plan to them, with their proposed role and the kind of commitment they are being asked to make.

When the recruitment is complete, a group meeting, preferably a dinner, is held for a leisurely, in-depth discussion of the whole plan and procedure.

Training

Bible Study

These people are not to go out just to induce people to join the church, the failing of so much of the post–World War II visitation. They are to discuss the faith with people of highly divergent knowledge of and experiences with the Christian faith and the church. They must, then, have a solid grasp of basic biblical truths. Enthusiasm to get started must be tempered with sound preparation.

As will be seen, these apostles (the "sent forth") will be on their own to discuss in depth Christian truth. They will need to answer both serious and captious questions, and to speak about the faith in a logical manner.

The Bible study should give a solid feel for:

1. God's plan in creation
2. Humanity's introduction of alienation
3. God's plan for reconciliation of individuals and society
4. Jesus' role in the plan of redemption
5. The critical state of humanity—individual and corporate
6. The role of the church
7. The role of individual Christians
8. The nature of the commitment.

The summary of faith statements in chapter 7, "Dealing with Deep Spiritual Truths," should be helpful, although not considered comprehensive. This study should involve extensive discussion among the group.

How to Make the Call

The visitors are trained for making assigned calls on people who are on the church's responsibility list, which is to say, assigned by the Holy Spirit through some circumstance. A call may produce immediate action, or it may be the beginning of a long, patient spiritual adventure.

The teams are carefully matched for balance. A slightly reticent person may be paired with a more outgoing one. Normally two men would not be assigned to call on women, or two women to call on men. Couples calling on couples is a recommended procedure. Conditions such as a team member's being in the same occupation or being from the same hometown as a person visited may be guiding factors. Sensitivity and alertness are the key.

A. Getting Acquainted, if Necessary

It is often advisable to schedule the visit by a prior telephone call. The person(s) will then have acceded to the call and know it is from the church. The visitors, then, have only to introduce themselves.

If not already acquainted, they use this mutual introduction period to establish a relaxed atmosphere. They do what comes naturally in any social visit to a home, remembering, however, that in this case they may have to make the hosts feel at ease. Care must be taken to avoid awkward or embarrassing questions. In the training session the group, knowing their community, should focus on questions that should be avoided. For instance, in a high unemployment area, questions about employment must be asked diplomatically.

The team proceeds, then, to learn more about their hosts. Where they are from, how long they have been in the community, and questions about their children help to dissolve apprehensions on the part of the hosts while the visitors establish themselves as just friendly people. Possible openers might be:

"We are glad to note that you worshiped with us on _____ [date]."

"We have been pleased to have your children in the vacation school [scouts, etc]."

"You graciously gave information to our canvass workers recently."

B. Getting to the Subject

We noted earlier the wide and intimidating variety of personal situations that have to be faced. They will range from some who need only be invited to those who will consume the evening venting their hostilities.

The introductory period should not be hurried, but on the other hand the visitors should not dally. The hosts know that there is an agenda ahead.

There is no "game plan." Some evangelistic strategies have a set of leading questions by which they seek to move the conversation to their desired end. Our conversations also have desired ends, but we are interested in real intercommunication with the hosts, not just skillfully manipulating them from one point to the next. It is conversation, dialogue, not a lawyer stating a case. Thus it is possible only to lay out some general ideas and illustrative situations. The helpful literature of the earlier movement is largely unavailable. The local leadership is on its own to seek the guidance of the Spirit in learning how to communicate the message.

The unapologetic purpose of the call is to encourage the person(s) to consider some level of commitment. Whether, when, or how to focus the conversation on a commitment is a judgment decision. Sensitivity and experience will show when the conversation should move toward a conclusion. The team must be sensitive as to when the conversation has reached its most progressive point and the limitation of this particular call. They hope for the ultimate—that the persons will eventually commit their lives to Christ and/or become a part of a Christian fellowship—but evaluating the conversation will suggest the best that they can hope for at that time.

In the continuing reflection sessions, teams will report on their experiences and how they dealt with various situations. This will be a learning process for all.

C. The Nature of the Conversation

Naturally the team leads the discussion, and one member should be designated in each particular case. The partner is alert to enter at strategic points, and the leadership may shift. Leadership does not signify control, but some effort at guidance.

Dialogue, in this case, begins by asking questions. It is necessary to understand something of the other's sense of Christianity and the church. The use of the question goes back to the garden, when the serpent asked Eve about their instructions. This was undoubtedly to get her asking herself "Why?" The serpent probably left her to stew over that for several days before making the attack. The use of the question is effective, not only when initiating the conversation, but throughout. It may often be strategic, instead of making a categorical statement, to say, "How do you think about this?"

There can be no game plan because of the variety of life settings. The hosts may be talkative or noncommunicative. They may be interested or lackadaisical, positive toward religion or hostile.

Information from the files, or sensed in the early conversation, may give the lead. If there is no information on earlier church relationship, a leading question may concern their history or attitude toward Christianity and the church. The response may give a lead for the next move. If something negative emerges, one does not enter into an argument, but asks further questions to give the person a chance to expand. Then a response such as "Have you considered . . ."? can tactfully enter another point of view. At some point a team member may say, "Would you be interested in how I see that?" The team seeks graciously to show another side to the negativity.

Team members will realize that whether the negative experiences expressed were real or merely perceived, they are real in the minds of their conversationalists. Jesus acknowledged the reality of the Temple controversy. His response, however, was to move the discussion to a higher level. It is an art for visitors.

There may be biblical questions raised. Care must be taken to sense whether they are genuine or like the gentleman's question we mentioned earlier in this chapter about, "Lead us not into temptation." The team will not let itself get bogged down in useless controversy over trivial matters.

In many instances there will be people who have neither knowledge of nor experience with the church or scripture. One member should give a thumbnail sketch of basic Christian truth, brief and concise, and then receive questions about it. Inquiry should be made of their interest in a Bible study class. This probably should not be the adult Bible class on Sunday morning, but a setting where the curriculum is the basic truths. In small situations it might be well for a church leader to lead several study sessions, either at home or at the church, so that they might receive some directed study. In other situations, there may be several such people, and a study group can be organized.

If there are children, their lives and welfare may be the focus. The get-acquainted questions may have given a clue that the parents were reared in active Christian homes. "You indicated that you grew up in a Christian home. How do you feel about such an environment for your children?" Or, "Your children are growing up in very dangerous moral settings. Have you thought about their need for sound spiritual training?"

These are but the barest suggestive skeletons of how God's messengers may be effective in this ministry. Many lessons will be learned in "on-the-job training."

D. Dealing with Problem Situations

These take such a variety of forms that praying for the guidance of the Spirit may be the best preparation. However, in the training some of them may be identified and discussed beforehand. Others will emerge in report meetings and be analyzed. Some common ones are that a person:

Had a negative experience in some church

Was forced to go to church school and church as a child

Believes the church is only after money

Thinks the church meddles too much in the affairs of the world

Considers that the church is just concerned with "pie in the sky by and by," with no concern for people's daily lives and problems

Believes the churches are too split up

Thinks one can be just as good a Christian without belonging to a church (this seems to be a major objection with many "baby boomers")

The training prepares for all such objections and adds others as they are experienced.

E. How to Bring the Conversation to a Focus

As said above, the unapologetic purpose is to encourage the hosts to some form of commitment. Acknowledgment was made that, while full commitment to Christ is the ultimate goal, the outcome of any particular call may be something far short of that. The options may include any of the following:

To accept Jesus as Savior and plan to join the church

To reaffirm faith and unite with the church

To transfer membership to the church

To reactivate a former church membership

To unite with some other church of choice—possibly wife's or husband's church

To join a study group

To have the pastor visit

To come to worship the following Sunday

To worship again soon

To receive another team visit

These, of course, do not exhaust the options, but illustrate how the visit seeks a decision or opens the door for further patient work.

It is important to stress that if the conversation suggests, the hosts be encouraged to unite with some other church. Visitors represent Christ, not just the particular church. This breadth of spirit inevitably elevates the visiting church in their minds, as they sense that concern is for them, not the institution.

The object of the visit is to make as much progress as is possible toward a positive decision for Christ and the church. There should be no compulsion to get a decision, which would encourage a hard sell. It is often the beginning of a long-term relationship, in which the Holy Spirit may use a variety of people and experiences.

The team does seek some commitment. The process of an earlier time used a commitment card that those who expressed a first or renewed commitment or desire to take steps to unite with a church were asked to sign if they chose. For some this may seem too manipulative. But the purpose of the call is to seek some level of commitment, and the leadership should determine how it should be confirmed.

After leaving each home, the team should review briefly the visit and make notes for the report.

Report Meetings

There should be a rough time set for the report meeting the same evening or Sunday, as the case may be. With the unpredictability of visits, flexibility is necessary. One team may have found someone at home at only one place, and found that to be only a brief visit. Another may have got into a deep and meaningful discussion and judged it unwise to break it off. The Spirit still blows where it wills, and we cannot time it. A team may need to call in and suggest that the meeting proceed without them.

The report meetings are strategic. Everybody rejoices at positive reports. Everybody shares in the concerns of those who found their communication unpleasant. Reporting back to the reflection session, a team that has spent the time with a hostile situation should not report a failed visit. The venting might well be a therapeutic experience for the ventor, a beginning of communication. This is patient work. The group discusses the tactics of teams and together sees what all can learn. Adequate records are made for future planning. Prayers at the end are natural and fervent.

What next? Each team tries to end a visit with the door open for themselves or someone else to call later.

Where decisions for Christ and/or the church are made, the church follows up with necessary steps.

Where further cultivation is the need, plans are made to follow up. Often the visit of the pastor is the next needed step. The team should try to get people's assent to such a visit.

Each team makes written reports on its visits that are recorded in the prospects' files. In most cases when a visit was inconclusive, teams should suggest how soon another visit should be made. One situation may be very promising, suggesting an early follow-up. Another may need time for the Spirit to work unaided. A problem situation unveiled may suggest a gentle inquiry as to whether the family would like for the pastor or some other person with counseling skills to come as a counselor.

Meanwhile, other forms of communication continue, gentle and loving reminders that the church is there and that it cares.

Jesus had limited time with Ms. Samaritan. The time we will have to witness to any particular person is indeterminate, but we need to work as though there were no tomorrow. It is not only that death is unpredictable, but that God has something valuable for each person for daily living and urgent work for that person to be about. And the longer the wait, the more difficult it may be to respond. Paul told the Corinthians, "See, now is the acceptable time; see, now is the day of salvation!" (2 Cor. 6:2).

In the church served by the writer there were several hundred people on the responsibility list. All of them were open-ended but one. A woman asked that we not bother her anymore. Her name was removed from the work list to the prayer list.

Evangelism is patient work!!

7

EVANGELISM IS DEALING WITH DEEP SPIRITUAL TRUTHS

If ever there was an unlikely character for discussing deep spiritual truths, Ms. Samaritan qualified. Jesus' description of her marital life, culminating in an unmarried liaison, does not suggest a domestic setting in which spiritual matters had high priority. And since she drew her water at noon to avoid contact with the village women, one cannot imagine her braving the stares at the synagogue.

Then, the setting was not conducive either. The well at midday was more often a meeting place for very nonspiritual purposes, and both Jesus and she knew it. Introducing spiritual matters in such a setting could be quite problematical. Fluent church school teachers may find themselves speechless away from the church setting. Even many ministers find it awkward to discuss spiritual matters in a nonsupportive environment, but there are more contacts to be made away from the church than on its premises. Many with whom we should be conversing will feel much more open on their own territory. The church person who can feel at ease with a Coke in a "happy hour" setting discussing spiritual matters has established a spiritual beachhead. And the majority of people will never be on our turf until we have effectively met them on theirs. As noted, Jesus just might well have planned this nonliturgical classroom.

In the case of the Samaritan woman, moreover, tradition was working against this kind of relationship for spiritual teaching. According to Dr. Kenneth Bailey, rabbinic tradition said that to teach Torah to a woman was like teaching her lechery.[1] Not only was Jesus forbidden

---

[1]Kenneth Bailey, personal correspondence to the author.

by custom to talk to her, he was forbidden by that tradition to teach her religious things under any circumstance.

Jesus obviously ignored this tradition consistently. The teaching that he did privately in the home of Mary and Martha he also did in public, as the crowds described were composed of women and children as well as men (Matt. 14:21). This was one of the reasons for the bitter hostility of the religious leaders. But the well was an even more far-out classroom!

To open the conversation in this situation, with all its handicaps, Jesus used a simple but effective didactic approach. He started with the subject at hand—water. It was a natural subject in that setting. It put them on common ground and helped her to be at ease. She was also at ease because there was no reason for her to suspect that any profound truth was on the way.

"Deep spiritual truths" does not imply complicated theological formulations. Jesus left those for the apostle Paul and the succession of "Pauls" through the centuries. Skimming through a red-letter edition of the Gospels, one will find for the most part that Jesus spoke those eternal verities in simple language and illustrated them with pictures from everyday life. He spoke of a farmer planting his field, of a woman who had lost a coin, of a shepherd and his sheep, of strained and restored relations between a father and son.

Even in talking to a religious leader like Nicodemus, Jesus talked about birth and the wind blowing through the trees.

This is not to imply that wrestling with the profound implications of Christian truth is not essential. Those profound theological concepts may be compared to a huge hydroelectric plant. The plant is necessary to produce huge concentrations of electric power. But step-down transformers are necessary to convert it into usable strengths to operate our household gadgets. Some persons need to be plugged into that high-voltage theology. They then function as transformers to interpret that truth in manageable units for everybody.

Persons who explain the gospel to children, whether in a class, in sermons, or as parents in the home, learn an excellent discipline for evangelism. Since evangelism is introducing people to the faith, it must start where they are.

Deep Truth—
the Water of Life

Jesus not only uses the drink of water to start the conversation, he makes it the focus. The first major truth he shares with Ms. Samaritan is that for her needs there is an always available, completely satisfying supply. She doubly does not understand. First, naturally, she thinks he is talking about physical water. Second, very reasonably, she does not believe he can do what she thinks he is saying. Only after the conversation is over, after she has run into town with her story about a man at the well, after the villagers have gone to the well and returned—only in the quiet of the evening, when she muses over the incredible events of the day, would the meaning really dawn on her: "He was telling me that he has something to meet the needs that I have tried to meet in so many ways that didn't work!" God does have answers to the needs built into the nature of humanity.

God's world has so many natural matches that belie the "creation by accident" idea.

The ear is matched by vibrations, made incidentally by a passing car or intentionally by a spoken word or the playing of music.

The eye is matched by light, form, color, a smile, or printed characters that speak.

The skin has sensitivities that enjoy the warmth of the spring sun, but that sound warnings of intense heat or damaging cold.

Hunger is matched with food and, as in our story, thirst with water.

The Creator who designed a multitude of physical "matches" created persons with spiritual, psychological, and emotional needs and provided what is needed to properly satisfy them. Evangelism is not seeking to introduce something extraneous into lives; it is seeking to connect the needs of persons, whether perceived or not, with God's prescient provision for those needs. It realizes that just as hunger and thirst are functions to serve bodily needs, and skin sensations and elevated temperatures serve as needed warnings, God provides spiritual hungers, thirsts, and danger signals. "Blessed are those who hunger and thirst for righteousness, for they will be filled" (Matt. 5:6).

Paul Tournier ascribes the awareness of needs to an awareness of Christianity.

> But at the bottom of his soul he preserves an ideal and a conception of life which he owes to Christianity; the idea of a divine law, qualms of conscience when he violates it, fear of punishment, the need for pardon, grace and reconciliation with God and man, the yearning for a complete renewal of his being, and at the same time for personal fulfillment and fellowship with others. Indeed he has received all these ideas from God himself through the teaching of the church; and therefore he cannot erase them from his consciousness.[2]

Tournier is correct in saying that in our society many people have been directly or indirectly touched by the Christian faith and teachings and the omnipresent church. Beyond that, however, there are many who have had minimal or no contact with what Tournier describes, but who have the inherent, that is, God-given, needs for which God has provided the supply. This is patently true with the carrying of the gospel to other cultures, but there are "pagans" in our own society with no awareness of God or the church. They too have the yearnings and longings that open them to the depth of Christian truth.

Faith in God includes faith that when we communicate with a person, the Holy Spirit is there ahead of us. It is believing that in many instances there is active wishing or passive waiting. The question is whether we become the messengers.

Flowers and grasses mature in the fall and drop seeds, which lie dormant until the warmth of spring and the presence of adequate moisture cause them to germinate. Planting the seed and germination may be widely separated in time, and the harvest even more so. Unrealized needs and even realized ones may take frustratingly long to reach out for what God offers. Our task is to sow the seed and do our part under the direction of the Spirit to provide the warmth and moisture that will in time stimulate germination.

We have quoted in chapter 3 from Isaiah and his call to the hungry and thirst to come and get the good bread and water free.

---

[2]Paul Tournier, *The Whole Person in a Broken World* (New York: Harper & Row, 1981).

A familiar hymn voices the response:

> I heard the voice of Jesus say,
> "Behold, I freely give
> The living water; thirsty one,
> Stoop down and drink, and live."
> I came to Jesus, and I drank
> Of that life-giving stream;
> My thirst was quenched, my soul revived,
> And now I live in him.
>
> (Horatius Bonar)

The Truth— about God and Worship

When Jesus described her life situation and Ms. Samaritan got uncomfortable, she sought to divert the conversation by starting a religious argument. As Jesus used the ready subject of water to share a deep spiritual truth, he now capitalizes on the subject she raises: where to worship. Whether she worshiped at all would be open to question, but Jesus does not expose that as he did her marital life. Rather, he responds by lifting the subject to a higher level. Instead of responding argumentatively, as she expects, he talks with her seriously, showing that the important thing is not where you worship but whom and how you worship. Again, to this unlikely student and, through her to us, he gives profound truths about God and worship.

In a few words (though we must remember that John's account is but a digest of the conversation), he dispenses with any need for concern over the place of worship. Kenneth Bailey says, "We no longer need any geography for our prayers."[3] He notes that freedom of Christianity from geography would have prevented the tragedy of the Crusades and the long festering aftermath to this day. Worship is relational, not spatial.

That same broom stroke swept away times and modes of worship— things that have caused tragic divisions in the body of Christ.

With three words, "God is spirit," Jesus does away with the God of

---

[3]Bailey, personal correspondence with the author.

physical characteristics, the patriarchical God, the God who loses his temper. A profound truth given to a peasant villager, whose life did not recommend her as a recipient!

A Deep Truth—
"I Am He"

Jesus' telling her the third deep spiritual truth is amazing, because he shared it so stingily. When, thrown into a pensive, reflective mood by Jesus' serious conversation, there come floating back to her as in a dream words of long ago, she murmurs, "I know that Messiah is coming. . . . When he comes, he will proclaim all things to us," Jesus replies, "I am he!" (John 4:25–26). To this woman—a truth that he hardly entrusted to the disciples!

Jesus, here and elsewhere, gave profound truths to all sorts of people. He presented them in simple terminology and illustrated them by pictures from everyday life. And "the large crowd was listening to him with delight" (Mark 12:37).

Truths Essential
for Evangelism

Evangelism is sharing deep spiritual truths. The volume of spiritual truth is massive. The truths are also controversial, as witnessed by the fact that interpretations of scripture have created ecclesiastical divisions and even caused executions. But there is a compendium of truth—the basic essentials for understanding the Christian faith in order to accept or reject it. The ambassador for Christ must have a clear grasp of those essentials and how they relate, in order to be able to communicate effectively. The church, with all that it has to teach, must keep in focus the basics that must be grasped and accepted in order to make a sound commitment.

The early church, living in the afterglow of the resurrection, in what was believed to be a brief transition before Christ's return, had as its creed only the affirmation "Jesus is Lord." This was, however, no simple intellectual assent. Under Roman rule, all sorts of religions were permitted as long as one thing was remembered: Caesar was god! To claim any other as god was treason, punishable by death. "Jesus is Lord," then, was truly a life commitment. Acceptance of Jesus as Lord of one's life should be done as seriously as the commitment of those who risked Caesar's wrath.

Developments during the intervening centuries, however, have greatly confused what is fundamental truth. This is both cause and effect of the atomization of the church, with variations of belief ranging from minor issues to those that raise questions as to whether some can justly be called "Christian." These varying and ofttimes hostile claims of truth can be confusing to the learner.

The sheer mass of theological interpretation makes it necessary that, for the seeker, we isolate from the accretions of the centuries and the scholars the basic truths that are essential for making a commitment. The rest of life will be a growing grasp of the truth.

However, due to the fact that many people have already been exposed to ideas about the faith—some right, some wrong—the agents of the Spirit must be ready to respond cogently, clearly, and coherently to their questions and concerns.

In the early nineteenth century some Christians sought to solve both the theological and the ecclesiastical problems by "returning to the early church." They felt that if they could just shuck off the theological and ecclesiastical accretions of the centuries, they would have a church that all could accept, and could thus reunify the church. That did not work, and their work resulted in just another denomination. But their effort illustrates the problem of differentiating between basic Christian truths and theological assumptions.

Sharing the truth of the gospel is also confused by "church membership"; becoming disciples of Christ is confused with "joining the church." The unhealthy growth of the post–World War II period was merely a highly accentuated phase of a continuing church malady: mere recruitment of members, not evangelism. As noted in an earlier chapter, in that instance the church had a rich opportunity. The personal, national, and world traumas had left people searching. In large part the church failed them by not bringing to them the depths of spiritual truth and by settling for church membership. It was a tragic betrayal of Christ, of the church, and of people. When they were seeking for bread we may not have given them stones (see Matt. 7:9), but we gave too many of them junk food instead of the truth—the bread of life. And thousands of them drifted away . . . still hungry.

Membership in what seems to be an effective social organization can easily be assumed without mental or spiritual stress. Committing one's life to Christ, even for one who has grown up within the faith community, demands reevaluation of one's life and priorities that, while not approximating the trauma of Paul's conversion, should not be merely a *pro forma* act. The profound and demanding truth of the gospel has to be made clear.

A Basic Truth—
the Bible Is the Word of God

A deadly weakness in many Christian lives is an indifference to, a lack of interest in, and ignorance of the Holy Scriptures.

People who are physically malnourished are susceptible to attacks of disease. The spiritually malnourished are vulnerable to temptation.

The physically underfed do not have the energy to do the work they need to do. The spiritually malnourished do not have the spiritual strength to meet the challenges of living the Christian life.

A basic truth for evangelism is that the scriptures are the Word of God, to be studied, believed, and used as a guide for life.

The prereception, Baptism instruction should stress this fact. The "continuing education" that should be provided to every member should be so biblically based that the Bible is integral to the member's life. The wider church must provide help with materials and methods for teaching the Word of God.

Care should be taken to clarify the progressive nature of God's revelation. Otherwise, reading the ofttimes primitive and cruel events of the Old Testament may well ruin the effort to understand the scripture. It must be seen as God's bringing a people from a primitive stage to the more spiritually refined stage in which the moral and ethical teachings of Jesus might be rooted.

A serious weakness emerges here. Few congregations have thoughtful, well-organized, continuing Bible study programs. As a synod staff worker, meeting with many sessions, I became aware that many elders have slight grasp of scripture. They are not, therefore, likely to lead the church in developing and maintaining solid scriptural study programs.

A Basic Truth—God

Nowhere does the Bible state that there is God, or seek to prove God. It merely declares that "In the beginning . . . God created." The magnificence and intricacy of the universe can be evidence of the Creative Mind. When we look at a watch, a lighted electric bulb, or an airplane, we would consider foolish any person who claimed that they "just happened." The matched needs and resources examined earlier are evidence of a creative mind. But when all the evidence has been examined, there must still be the "leap of faith" that there is God.

However, believing that there is a God is not the faith of the gospel. The faith that Christians live by is faith *in* God. It is not a historical acceptance, but a personal trust. Idiomatically speaking, it is betting our lives on God and God's way.

The physical evidence of a creative God might witness to a God of power. Scripture witnesses to a God of love. The message of evangelism is: "God is love" and "God loves you."

Basic Fact—
Creation of a Good World

A loving God created the world to be a good world. Whatever the process that science seeks to describe, Genesis portrays a God creating purposefully, carefully, lovingly. Science seeks to discover the process, but science cannot preside over its own birth.

A recurring refrain in the Genesis 1 narrative is, "God saw that it was good." The wonder of the created world, so many aspects of which work right or can be seen to have been created to work right, testifies to a loving Creator. There are certainly unanswered problems, such as typhoons, earthquakes, and other phenomena that cannot be blamed on human misuse of nature, but the mass of evidence is for a world meant to be good.

A key to understanding the nature of the world God intended is found in two biblical statements. One is "God is love," as noted above.

The other is: "God created humankind in his image, in the image of God he created them" (Gen. 1:27). Thus human life was to be lived out as and in love.

The God of creation is also the God of redemption.

Basic Fact—
Humankind Rejected God's Love

The inevitable question is: "What happened to God's meant-to-be-good world?" People ask why God permits such rampant evil in life, and especially when it vents itself on the innocent and helpless. What "happened" is so intrinsically part of the divine-human tragedy that the account of it follows immediately the account of creation. Humankind rebelled against the way God meant for the world to work, frustrating God's design and causing progressive suffering for itself and even for the creation.

To love God would be to live in obedience, and humankind chose to reject God and love. Terrestrial gravitation draws all bodies in the earth's sphere toward the center. Without it, we can only assume that heavenly bodies would fly, uncontrolled, outward into space. Love is the cohesive force intended to hold humans in proper relationships. Rejecting love as the principle of life, humans substituted the centrifugal forces of selfishness for the centripetal force of love. But God gave humans free will.

God promised death for disobedience (Gen. 2:15–17). The tempter contradicted, and promised that by going on their own, people would "be like God, knowing good and evil" (Gen. 3:4–5). Ironically, both were right. The sinners "knew good and evil," and that was the spiritual death that has cursed all humanity as succeeding generations have followed their pattern. The scurrying into the brush like frightened rabbits was symbolic of the separation from God—the death that was the wages of sin (Rom. 6:23). The universality and destructiveness of sin is a basic truth, causing much of the evil and suffering in the world.

Satan's half-truth in the garden is repeated endlessly as succeeding generations find rationalizations that prevent their grappling with the fact of their sin. Many psychologists and psychiatrists explain away sin psychologically, and social scientists find environmental explanations to remove guilt. But, like the hapless Humpty-Dumpty, "All the king's horses and all the king's men couldn't put Humpty together again." Sartre's title states the human predicament—*No Exit*.

The truth that must be faced in order for God's redemptive love to work is that human life is infested and infected with sin; all participate in it and are guilty. The garden story is but a mythological statement of the saga of humanity. An essential step toward redemption is to realize that one shares the common sin of humanity.

Sin sets in motion a chain reaction of alienations. The primary one, noted above, is alienation from God. But there follows an escalation of alienations, a "chain-reaction crack-up." For instance, in the garden story we can be sure that each member of the couple henceforth endured bitter, remorseful self-hatred. There was alienation within. Alienated from God, there was no "balm in Gilead to make the wounded whole, . . . to heal the sin-sick soul." Growing understanding of the nature of human nature has revealed something of the destructiveness of self-hatred.

Adam would always remember that Eve took the initiative in the miserable story. On the other hand, Eve could never forget Adam's scornful, accusing finger in her face when God asked him what had happened. This is symbolic of omnipresent interpersonal alienations that can make life an earthly hell. That the first home produced a fratricide is a not unpredictable outcome.

The sin of alienation is a poison in the personal and corporate bloodstream of humankind. That toxin, with no antitoxin, is not only poisonous to the self, it poisons relations with other people and the society.

The Tower of Babel story (Gen. 11:1–9) represents alienation in the social structure. Men (*sic*) set out to do something that they thought was for their own good. But their expressed goals were selfish—pride and security. "Come, let us build ourselves a city, and a tower with its top in the heavens, and let us make a name for ourselves; otherwise we shall be scattered abroad upon the face of the whole earth" (Gen. 11:4). The story gives God credit for the stultifying breakdown of communication, but the breakdown was built into human nature. Selfish motivations preclude harmonious living and working together. Thus we see selfishness extruding itself into human society. We see the society poisoned.

This absence of love invades even the church. When the members of the church board are striving for power and prestige, the church suffers. Personal exhibitionism can ruin the ministry of the choir. Any unity in the church can be destroyed by personal ambition and pride.

Honesty in explaining spiritual truths demands that we make it clear to potential Christians and church members that they would be entering an imperfect community.

Only recently have we come to learn that sin brought alienation with the created universe. A few years ago fifteen hundred top scientists—many of them Nobel laureates—sounded a doleful warning that humankind has a threatening date with destiny, in which within possibly as little as a decade the point of no return on the destruction of the earth's livability might be passed. An ignorant greed and ambition began the process, but more recently, knowing that the air and water are increasingly toxic, we continue an undeclared war against nature. And nature is fighting back.

Alienation is from God, self, other people, in the social structure and against humankind's earthly home. Understanding the gospel demands understanding the truth about human sin and guilt and that no one is free from them. And the alienated have no resources to meet their own needs. We cannot interpret Christianity without helping people to grasp the reality and the nature of sin.

God's Plan B—
Redemption

A major truth is that God did not give up on humankind. God loved the world so much that God just could not. Alienation was promised, alienation as the result of disobedience. Humankind had earned and learned that alienation, and was in self-afflicted misery. God, who created patiently over unfathomable time, now began the long way back, a patient plan that would take centuries to evolve. It was a plan to dissolve alienation in reconciliation, to supplant selfishness with love.

The reversal of the result of the act of Adam and Eve began with another couple—Abraham and Sarah—from whom God developed a race of people. Over centuries, that people was led through stages of ethical and spiritual understanding to the point that they were ready to be the host people for God's intervention in the person of Jesus Christ. The Old Testament is the record of that spiritual odyssey.

The keystone message of scripture is that "Christ died for our sins" (1 Cor. 15:3 and passim). That is, he took on himself the wages that humanity had so assiduously earned—death. Since we have seen that that death was separation from God, there seem to have been two deaths on the cross. The second was when "Jesus, crying with a loud voice, said, 'Father, into your hands I commend my spirit'" and "breathed his last"(Luke 23:46). But that was a physical death. Already he had paid the penalty—the separation from God. In the agony of the crucifixion, with no earthly friend to help, when it all seemed too much to bear, Jesus turned to God; and, if the record is true, God wasn't there! Then Jesus uttered the most awe-full cry of human history: "My God, my God, why hast *thou* forsaken me?" (Mark 15:34, KJV). The eternal Son of God, in the dreadful and desperate time of his need, suffered the separation from God that humankind had deserved.

He himself had said, "God so loved the world that he gave his only Son, so that everyone who believes in him may not perish but may have eternal life" (John 3:16).

Speaking of his impending death, Jesus said, "Now my soul is troubled. And what should I say—'Father, save me from this hour'? No, it is for this reason that I have come to this hour" (John 12:27).

Paul puts redemption in terms of the alienation that humanity had caused:

> So if anyone is in Christ, there is a new creation: everything old has passed away; see, everything has become new! All this is from God, who reconciled us to himself through Christ, and has given us the ministry of reconciliation; that is, in Christ God was reconciling the world to himself, not counting their trespasses against them, and entrusting the message of reconciliation to us. So we are ambassadors for Christ, since God is making his appeal through us; we entreat you on behalf of Christ, be reconciled to God. For our sake [God] made him to be sin who knew no sin, so that in him we might become the righteousness of God. (2 Cor. 5:17–21)

There is no escaping it—the Christian faith is based on what we believe is historical fact: that Christ lived, died, rose again, and lives. Either because the church has not made that clear, or because they wanted to be members of the church regardless, there are many church members, and even ministers, who do not accept the basic facts of the faith. There are members who do not recite the creeds because they do not wish to say what they do not believe.

Facing this in his day, Paul wrote:

> For since, in the wisdom of God, the world did not know God through wisdom, God decided, through the foolishness of our proclamation, to save those who believe. For Jews demand signs and Greeks desire wisdom, but we proclaim Christ crucified, a stumbling block to Jews and foolishness to Gentiles, but to those who are the called, both Jews and Greeks, Christ the power of God and the wisdom of God. (1 Cor. 1:21–24)

Reconciliation is our opening to life, by the grace of God and the sacrifice of Jesus Christ.

Reconciliation is our commission, as we are called to be ambassadors for Christ.

Reconciliation is our message.

Reconciliation is a gift. In return for the gift, the reconciled gives self.

Redemption in Jesus Christ offers (1) peace with God, (2) peace with oneself, (3) peace with fellow human beings, and (4) the building blocks for peace in society.

Reconciliation with God is not, "Let's shake hands and make up." Reconciliation with God is saying and meaning, "O.K., God, I'll do it your way." It is removing self from the center of life and letting God take God's place there. The new center demands new priorities. It is truly a "conversion"—a radical change. Evangelism is helping others to understand what the love of God offers and how it can be received.

Peace with self is not satisfaction with self. We never reach a level of living that frees us from sinning. But in the restored relationship with God we are assured of God's forgiveness and our restoration and reconciliation.

"If we say that we have no sin, we deceive ourselves, and the truth is not in us. If we confess our sins, he who is faithful and just will forgive us our sins and cleanse us from all unrighteousness" (1 John 1:8–9).

However, since sin is ever with us, we do not experience a onetime cleansing. Repentance and forgiveness are daily experiences in the life of the Christian. Each morning's prayer is seeking strength and guidance for the day, and each evening's prayer includes seeking forgiveness for the day's failings.

Worship is one of God's gifts for the unceasing restoration of the human soul. We are constantly reminded of our need and of God's grace. In an experience that is both intellectual and emotional, we experience the cleansing of repentance and forgiveness, the encouragement that in Christ we can do better, and guidance as to how we can live in Christ.

Peace with self is a corollary of peace with God. Since God forgives us, we do not bear the demoralizing load of guilt that makes life a hell.

Peace with ourselves and our own shortcomings gives us new attitudes toward others. Knowing the love and grace of God in our own lives, we reach out to others in that spirit, so that love and grace may flow through us to others. Forgiven, we forgive. Interpersonal peace flows from peace with God and peace with self.

Evangelism is sharing the good news of our multiple reconciliations through the redemptive love of God in Jesus Christ.

The Church and the World

What is the church? Everybody will have some concept of what the church is, many of those concepts damaging and destructive. The person who protests that "there are too many hypocrites in the church" does not understand what the church is. The person who claims not to be good enough to join the church has a wrong concept of the church. Those who see the church as either just a route to heaven or just a worthwhile social agency have harmful ideas of the church. Several denominations suffer because of members and leaders who have deficient ideas of what the church is and what it should be doing.

It is important that the church be properly represented and interpreted. First, clear distinction must be made between giving one's life to Christ and becoming a member of the church. Otherwise it is fatally easy for persons to become organizational members with no commitment to Christ.

What the church is, is rooted in what has been quoted repeatedly here: "God so loved the *world*"; in Christ, God was reconciling the *world* to himself.

Needless, painful, and costly controversies range around the relationship of the church and the world, framed in the language of "evangelism versus church and society," personal salvation versus restoration of the human society God intended.

It was human sin that produced the brokenness and wretchedness of "the world," and now we see God working for the restoration of individuals for their own sake and to be agents for the restoration of the damaged society. God's plan of redemption includes the redemption of the good social structures that were inherent in God's creation. Those who claim that personal salvation is the one assignment of the church seem not to realize the problems inherent in "saving souls" in a corrupt and oppressive society. Effective personal salvation work is hampered and often thwarted by the society in which it is sought. Earlier reference was made to the necessity of fighting rats and fleas to stop the bubonic plague. Modern missionary medicine is largely ineffective in places where human excrement runs through open sewers and water is contaminated with deadly bacteria. Part of our task is developing the environment in which spirituality thrives. Thinking that there can be effective healing of people living in societies where there are no "spiritual public health" efforts runs counter to what our knowledge of human life and environments teaches us.

These two aspects of the mission represent two ways in which the love of God is expressed. The word must be validated by the work and the work must be overtly related to the word. "In the same way, let your light shine before others, so that they may see your good works and *give glory to your Father in heaven*" (Matt. 5:16, emphasis added).

Those sharing the gospel must needs grasp and share this truth; otherwise people enter the church unaware of the true nature and mission of the church. They envision it as either a "do good" social agency or a "Jacob's ladder" for a celestial climb. The result is frustration and disillusionment of people and life-killing controversy in the church.

A Christianity which has lost its vertical dimension has lost its salt and is not only insipid in itself, but useless for the world. But a Christianity which would use the vertical preoccupation as a means for escape from its responsibility for and in the common life of humanity is a denial of the incarnation of God's love for the world, manifested in Christ. The whole secret of the Christian faith is that it is humanity-centered because it is God-centered. (W. A. Visser 't Hooft, at the 1968 World Council of Churches Assembly)

A third-world Christian, discussing the resurgence of at least talk about evangelism in U.S. churches, said that he was afraid that it might be successful. Noting my expected puzzlement, he explained. What he fears is an inrushing of people who have a lifeless "civil religion," who cannot separate church from nation, or the cross from the flag.

Converts to Christianity who know the truth of the gospel and its implications in human life will know that the gospel sits in judgment on all human institutions and systems. They will be the salt of the earth, counteracting its putrefactions, purifying its life.

The Redeemed
Christian Life

As in many other facets of the gospel and church of Jesus Christ, people are led astray by what they think they know, by the often semipagan notions they have about Christianity. The evangelistic church and evangelistic messengers need to seek to make clear what the Christian life is and means.

"Salvation is free" is an old and true adage. But the truth is broader and deeper. Jesus Christ paid the debt in his double death on the cross. Redemption is offered free—there is no way we can earn it. But acceptance has its obligations. The cruel statement "a life for a life," dealing with capital punishment, has a different meaning in the message of evangelism. Christ has given his life for us; acceptance of that gift entails our giving our lives for/to him. There is no other way we can receive the gift.

Reference has been made to a new center and new priorities. Conversion means that we make a complete reversal: we cannot accept Christ and be the same. Living out the Christian life is the mandate of redemption.

The term "stewardship" describes the new relationship. It comes from old English life and language. Someone in a village took care of the pigs belonging to various families while they worked in the fields. He was called the "sty ward"—in charge, temporarily, of what belonged to someone else. Our lives always belonged to God; the difference is that we acknowledge God's ownership. We further acknowledge that Christ has redeemed us. Integrity in evangelism demands making it clear that the Christian life is quite contrary to customary standards of society.

A little boy made a boat, which he treasured greatly. Somehow it got away from him, but one day he saw it in a secondhand store. He told the owner how he had patiently made it. The owner told him that he could have it for what he had paid another little boy for it, which the boy paid gladly. Leaving the store he was saying, "Little boat, you're mine. You're twice mine—first I made you and now I've bought you." This little parable epitomizes the human-God relationship. The God who made us has redeemed us for God's self.

The Christian life is often confused with moral and ethical behavior, and it does demand the highest level of living. It is, however, far more than a code of ethics.

Nobody should ever "join the church" without its being made clear that it involves a surrender of self, with drastic ramifications. The Christian life is stewardship of time, of talents, of influence, of relationships, of possessions—in short, of all of life. Everything belongs to God and must be used at God's direction. Evangelism that does not make clear the implications of "accepting Christ" is false advertising and unscrupulous salesmanship.

Christian hymnody is full of expressions of this commitment:

> "Take My Life, and Let It Be Consecrated, Lord, to Thee"
>
> "Have Thine Own Way, Lord"
>
> "I Am Thine, O Lord"
>
> "Jesus Calls Us"
>
> "My Jesus, as Thou Wilt"
>
> "O Love That Wilt Not Let Me Go"
>
> "I Surrender All"

All are expressive of the life commitment of the Christian. Evangelism must say it!

A serious problem with witnessing to this truth is the poor testimony given by so many Christians. We are in danger of being in the "Do as I say, not as I do" trap. Even the congregation, with a self-serving, rather than a self-giving outreach, can be a negative witness.

It is certainly risky to select a few "basic truths," for so much of great importance is omitted. But this at least illustrates the essentials that the spokesperson for Christ must have deep hold on and be able to communicate. The circumstances of the communication will vary widely, for evangelistic conversation is tailored to the person in focus and that person's life situation. But, using the figure of the well, the agent for Christ needs to have a well of spiritual water from which to draw as opportunities appear. And, as anyone knows who has ever drawn water from a well, in order to draw out a bucketful, there has to be far more than a bucketful in the well.

Evangelism is sharing simple but profound truths, sharing them with earnestness and conviction, sharing them with humility and simplicity, to meet the situation at hand.

It is sharing them without judgment as to the other's ability to grasp them, but trusting the Holy Spirit to use what we do. It is truly faith and love in action when we share the deep spiritual truths of the gospel. It is telling the truth, although the result may be that of the wealthy young man of Matthew 19:16–22. The price was too great, and he went away. It is sharing the truth and letting that truth carry its own message.

8

EVANGELISM IS PASSIONATE, CONSUMING WORK

It had to happen eventually. The disciples had finished buying their provisions and were approaching the well. As they drew near enough to be sure they were seeing what they hoped they were not seeing, what were their reactions? Or more exactly, how did their consternation express itself? In a shocked silence? In hardly audible murmurs? Or, since we know that much later Peter still held on to some profanity, could someone have let loose an oath?

At the well, we can be sure that when Ms. Samaritan saw them approaching she suddenly became nervous and looked anxiously at Jesus, expecting him to quickly end the conversation. But, unperturbed, he talked leisurely on.

The disciples arrived and in a stunned silence began mechanically to prepare the meal. They knew Jesus too well to ask him why he was talking with her or to upbraid her for being there. But this time they knew that his unpredictability was all too predictable.

Finally there came a break in the conversation. She excused herself and, either forgetting her errand or not wanting to be slowed by carrying her water jar, she held up her long skirt and flew toward the village.

Absorbed in the intensity of the conversation, Jesus may well have been oblivious to the deathly silence around him. Then the silence was broken as someone announced that lunch was ready.

But the break in the tension was only momentary, for Jesus' next words threw them into consternation again. When he announced that he was not hungry, a puzzled mumbling began. "Has anyone brought him food?" Meaning, "Surely he hasn't eaten food that woman gave him!"

As noted earlier, dietary laws were among the strictest of Jewish laws. As Ms. Samaritan had pointed out, Jews and Samaritans did not share vessels in common. The barriers of race, religion, and custom that Jesus had ignored were trivial compared with eating food prepared by the wrong hands in the wrong way in the wrong vessels.

Jesus then mystified them with one of his puzzling statements: "I have food to eat that you do not know about." But he did not leave them wondering. "My food is to do the will of him who sent me and to complete his work. Do you not say, 'Four months more, then comes the harvest'? But I tell you, look around you, and see how the fields are ripe ["white," KJV] for harvesting." Was he waving toward some distant crops, or toward a crowd of Samaritans hurrying from the village?

The fields would have been of either wheat or barley, glistening in the sunlight, but as a farm boy reading this in the South, I visualized the expanses of cotton that challenged us from August into October— truly white! My siblings and I watched for the hot late summer sun to reach its zenith, which meant that we could take our weary bodies to the farmhouse, satisfy our ravenous hunger, and get a quick rest. But there were times when thunderclouds stood ominously in the south, and we knew that the cotton we did not get picked before the rains came would be beaten out of the bolls to the ground, dirtied, and greatly reduced in value. At such times our hunger and weariness were forgotten as we were absorbed in saving something of value.

We can believe that Jesus was so absorbed in the struggle of the soul of this woman that he was completely oblivious to his physical status. Even after the conversation had ended, his mind and spirit were still racing with the exhilaration of the spiritual encounter. Food was just not important.

He spoke passionately of the harvest. He saw Ms. Samaritan as the entry into the whole Samaritan people, and thus spoke of fields ready to be harvested. Today some would call that language of manipulation, but Jesus came to claim souls.

In view of Jesus' godly passion, a passionless Christian is an oxymoron—or worse. A passionless church is not "the body of Christ." Witnessing to God's love in Jesus Christ is not just "signing up customers."

It is a life-or-death, life-and-death business. Since God took the human predicament so seriously as to include the cross, human recipients of Christ's ministry must respond to God's passion with their own passion.

When a swimmer had rescued their child from drowning, the child's parents said, "Young man, if there is anything we can ever do for you, just let us know." With Christ and us there is no "if"; it is just, "Lord, tell us what you want us to do."

Humanity, made in the image of God—love—lost that image in its universal fall. Redeemed humanity is restored to that original nature. Passionate concern for others, then, is doing what comes naturally. If that is missing, we need to examine the nature of our own redemption.

Jesus calls us to passion: "If any want to become my followers, let them deny themselves and take up their cross and follow me" (Matt. 16:24).

John summarizes this subject succinctly:

Beloved, let us love one another, because love is from God; everyone who loves is born of God and knows God. Whoever does not love does not know God, for God is love. God's love was revealed among us in this way: God sent his only Son into the world so that we might live through him. In this is love, not that we loved God but that [God] loved us and sent his Son to be the atoning sacrifice for our sins. Beloved, since God loved us so much, we also ought to love one another. No one has ever seen God; if we love one another, God lives in us, and his love is perfected in us. (1 John 4:7–12)

Can there be such a thing as an indifferent Christian?

There is little evidence of passion in the lives of many churches and church members. Congregations seem quite satisfied with their "no business, as usual" lives. Like the church just up from our home, they are quite indifferent to outsiders like those of us along the street, who are physically neighbors but quite out of their world.

Tragically, the vast majority of church members fit the category of Joe described in chapter 2, who never thought during his years of working with Harvey to have any concern over the Christless nature of Harvey's life.

In chapter 2, on "Compulsion of Love," we noted the disappearance of saving lost souls from hell as a motive for evangelism and mission.

But, while not minimizing the eschatological hell, we noted that there are multiple earthly hells from which people need to be saved. Churches and Christians who have no agony over what is happening in the lives of people and society do not have in them the passionate love of God.

Our world is a frightening picture of wreckage and human spiritual and social carnage. The daily news is a daily horror story:

> Murders in and of families
>
> Children raped by parents
>
> Millions starving or grossly undernourished
>
> Genocide
>
> Brutal oppression and torture

The litany is long and shocking

And this is what has happened to God's good world.

Elsewhere we described God's built-in adjustment to inure humans against emotional devastation from watching pain and trauma. It works too well. As we live passionless lives, insulated against humanity's suffering, the divinity God breathed into us lies hidden under cold, gray ashes, needing the Spirit to blow it into flame.

Evangelism is eagerly calling people to the relationship with God that will:

> Make them part of the love chain
>
> Bring them into the fellowship of the body of Christ to help the prayer "Thy will be done on earth" to be realized
>
> Enable those who suffer from life's traumas to find in Christ the support they need for meeting life's crises
>
> Enable them to become part of the solution to humanity's problems rather than being part of the problem
>
> Help them, then, to work passionately at seeing that others share these experiences as they too become part of God's family

The evangelistic church engages in "business as usual," but business as usual is a passionate reaching out to those whom Jesus would reach. It is not a seasonal activity, but the everyday business of the church and its people.

For individual Christians, evangelism is a full-time job. They have, of course, to earn a living, carry out family responsibilities, and perform civic duties. But in carrying out all of these, relationships with family, friends, and colleagues are so suffused with a conscious concern for their spiritual welfare that it is comparable to Paul's admonition to "pray without creasing" (1 Thess. 5:17).

Evangelism is passionate, pervasive, and persistent.

9

EVANGELISM IS THE HOLY SPIRIT WORKING THROUGH PEOPLE

Evangelism is the work of the Holy Spirit, and people are the agents.

A family had a wonderful morning at the beach, enjoying all the things that make children fall in love with beaches. After lunch and naps, they went out again. To the dismay of the children, the tide had gone out and an uninteresting stretch of soggy sand lay before them. One of them cried, "Mommy, will it ever come back?", and was reassured, "Yes, it will come back."

With similar dismay, many Christians are looking at the dreary expanse and dismal quality of church and spiritual life and the somber statistical records, remembering exciting days and wondering, Will the tide of evangelism ever come back?

The ocean tides will come back, repeatedly and on schedule, because they are controlled by cosmic forces. Seaside recreation businesses can post information on high and low tides for their customers, because about every twelve hours and twenty-five minutes high tide will return.

True evangelism is also controlled by heavenly forces. Jesus established the working relationship when he said, "You will receive power when the Holy Spirit has come upon you; and [then] you will be my witnesses" (Acts 1:8).

We saw human beings at work in the well event. Jesus had given Ms. Samaritan good news.

He told her of the inexhaustible and efficacious provisions God had made for human spiritual needs.

He freed her from anxiety that her people's worship on Mount Gerizim was inherently deficient.

He told her that he was the Messiah for whom they had been looking and longing.

The human Jesus was the bearer of good news.

It was then her turn to be the bearer of good news.

So excited that she forgot her status in Sychar, she blurted out to the people what had happened at the well. And her utter sincerity gave her a strange credibility. But her witness was to the stranger at the well.

Evangelistic witnesses must have something that gives them credibility. There must be some glow in their lives, some aura of sincerity, some solid quality of life that reaches out to people. Like Peter and John before the council (Acts 4:13), they must be "recognized . . . as companions of Jesus."

Regardless of how glowing the witness's story may be, like Ms. Samaritan's it must point to Jesus. The villagers decided to go and see for themselves. Like Philip to Nathanael, the witness challenges others to "Come and see" (John 1:43–46).

Witnesses must trust the gospel message to speak for itself. One Easter morning I saw in the congregation a young man with whom we had been working for years. He had some intellectual difficulty with the church's message. One troubling instance lay in the long, painful cancer death of a young woman in the congregation. He could not see how a God both loving and powerful could allow such a thing to happen. I remember wishing that it were some other Sunday, when I did not have to present the unbelievable story of Easter. After the service I found him in my study. He said simply, "If what you said out there is what Christianity is about, I am ready." The message spoke for itself.

Believing that we are agents of the Holy Spirit equips us for our task. It gives us a humility that is needed to be effective witnesses. We know that we are agents being directed.

That same faith gives us courage. Facing difficult situations, we know that a power not of ourselves is at work. During the early part of World War II, Hitler had defeated Europe and England was nearly prostrate. It had lost its arms in France, and men were patrolling its beaches with hunting guns. Hitler had only to invade and all of Western Europe was his. Fortunately he did not know it. He chose instead to try to bomb England into submission, and failed. His war had been won, but the victory was lost.

With apologies for the analogy to something so beastly, I would show how the Holy Spirit has so often prepared a life for reception of the message; it remains only for the "ambassadors" (2 Cor. 5:20) to bring it. We cannot afford to be like Hitler and allow our fears, uncertainties, and inaction to immobilize us and thus lose God's victory.

As we work, study, and pray we have the realization of Christ's promise: "But the Advocate, the Holy Spirit, whom the Father will send in my name, will teach you everything, and remind you of all that I have said to you" (John 14:26). Jesus keeps his promise as the Holy Spirit guides us as agents of the Divine.

God says, as Jesus said to Peter, "On this rock I will build my church, and the gates of Hades will not prevail against it" (Matt. 16:18). Believing that the Holy Spirit is with us and goes before us, we can, with humility and courage, carry God's message to people who are as unlikely customers as Ms. Samaritan and Nicodemus.

As we respond to the celestial power, the tide of evangelism will come back. We need only to scan the history of the Christian church to see how the light of the church has at times seemed to flicker almost into extinction. Then the Holy Spirit, using some person, persons, or galvanizing event, has fanned that flicker into a consuming flame.

The event at the well gives us clues as to how it might happen.

Under the compulsion of God's love charging through human life, people will go out of their way to express that love.

Impassioned with the love of all humanity, they will ignore human barriers to carry that love across the street, across town, across the world.

Knowing God's patience with themselves, they will work with infinite patience.

Committed to God's truth, they will live it and teach it.

They know that they are Christ's witnesses because "the Holy Spirit has come upon [them]," and they are willing to witness to everyone, everywhere.

Evangelism is . . . will be . . . when those things happen.